THE
SOLDIER

Bath · New York · Cologne · Melbourne · Delhi
Hong Kong · Shenzhen · Singapore

CONTENTS

Front endpaper This defining image of World War I shows British troops marching toward frontline trenches near Ypres, October 1914.

Back endpaper Heavily armed soldiers of Israel's Givati Brigade prepare for an amphibious exercise in February 1991, demonstrating how marching remains relevant even in an age of mechanization.

▼ With far less technology and kit, but very similar fieldcraft tactics, Australian soldiers use a smoke screen to disguise an attack in November 1939.

INTRODUCTION

In popular understanding, and in the stirring battle scenes of many Hollywood movies, the defining moment of military service is found in combat. At this point, soldiers confront their fears of death and violence head-on, discovering whether they are able to survive the event physically and cope with it mentally. It is certainly true that combat is a seminal event in a soldier's career, a psychological landmark that can dominate his or her memory—sometimes destructively so—for the remainder of their lives. It is also true that for many professional soldiers, as opposed to conscripts, the opportunity to go to war is soberly pursued, as they willingly enter an arena in which hard-won skills are put to the ultimate test.

This picture of soldiering, however, is incomplete and selective. Looking back through history, millions of soldiers have experienced extended periods of active service, particularly in prolonged conflicts such as the Napoleonic Wars of the 19th century and the two World Wars of the 20th century. Yet for the vast majority of troops, the actual time spent fighting is a tiny fraction of their overall military career. Indeed, it is important to remember that soldiers continue to serve during peacetime, many going an entire and lengthy term in uniform without seeing any active service at all. Furthermore, we should also note that within armies the proportion of frontline combat troops has been consistently decreasing in relation to rear-echelon and support staff for much of the last century. In World War I, combat troops accounted for about 40 percent of the total manpower deployed into frontline action; in today's technologically reliant armies the figure is usually closer to 5 percent.

Pointing out these facts is by no means intended to diminish the place of combat in a soldier's life, or in the historical traditions of the armed services. This book addresses the day-to-day experience of battle, from soldiers opening paper musket cartridges with their teeth to coping with the psychological threat of improvised explosive devices (IEDs) in modern war zones. However, we also address key questions about the broader historical experience of soldiering. Where did the soldier come from, and how was he recruited? What sort of accommodation housed him, both in his home regions and when abroad on campaign? What were the factors affecting the soldier's health? What did he do when off duty? What roles did animals, such as horses and dogs, play in his life? What uniform did he wear, and what equipment was important to him?

By addressing these, and countless other questions, we are able to build up a fuller picture of what it is to be a soldier, from the mid-18th century to the present day, the era of standing armies. The picture we shall construct is one of continuity but also, inevitably, change. The continuities lie primarily in the realities of human physiology and psychology. Soldiers always need feeding, clothing, sheltering, and arming, and their mental requirements for morale, unit confidence, rest, and entertainment also have to be met. These needs are the same today as they have always been. What has changed—and profoundly so—is the technology wrapping itself around the soldier, plus the culture unique to each age. This book is therefore as much of a journey through the mental outlook of the soldier, as it is an examination of the things he has carried, worn, and experienced.

▶ French Army infantry talking with Zouaves (French colonial light infantry) at a Crimean War camp near Sevastopol in the 19th century. Note the difference between the traditional, colorful Zouave uniforms and the more modern, muted uniforms of the regular infantry.

GLOBAL CONFLICT AND REVOLUTION

MANY MILITARY HISTORIANS REGARD THE 17TH AND 18TH CENTURIES AS THE TRUE BEGINNINGS OF MODERN WARFARE. DURING THIS BLOODY PERIOD, FIREPOWER CAME OF AGE, FINALLY DISPLACING STEEL AS THE DECIDER OF BATTLES. COMMAND AND CONTROL BECAME EVER MORE IMPORTANT, AS EMPIRES AND NATIONS FOUGHT ONE ANOTHER IN NEAR-GLOBAL CONFLICTS, AND THE HUMBLE SOLDIER BECAME A PAWN IN EPIC POWER STRUGGLES.

◄ The French *Grande Armée* was, under the command of Napoleon, one of the most successful military forces in history. Here, flags and banners are raised by French soldiers following victory at the Battle of Austerlitz on December 2, 1805.

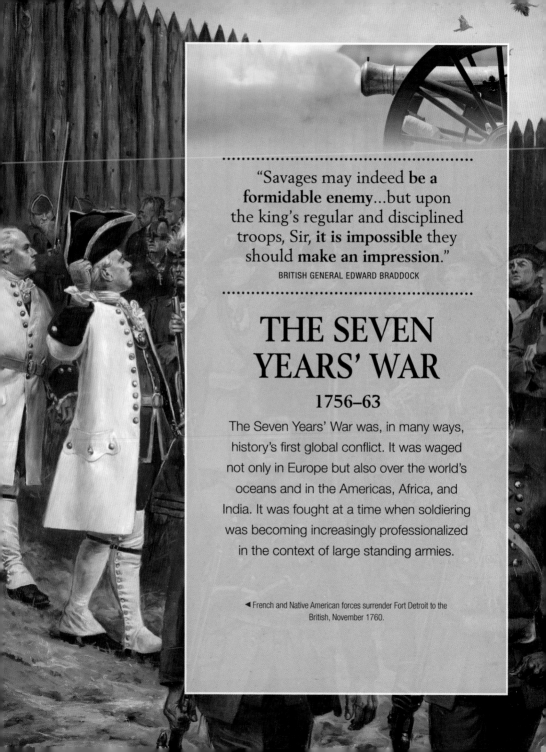

> "Savages may indeed **be a formidable enemy**...but upon the king's regular and disciplined troops, Sir, **it is impossible** they should **make an impression.**"
>
> BRITISH GENERAL EDWARD BRADDOCK

THE SEVEN YEARS' WAR

1756–63

The Seven Years' War was, in many ways, history's first global conflict. It was waged not only in Europe but also over the world's oceans and in the Americas, Africa, and India. It was fought at a time when soldiering was becoming increasingly professionalized in the context of large standing armies.

◄ French and Native American forces surrender Fort Detroit to the British, November 1760.

EMPIRES COLLIDE

The Seven Years' War was a politically complex conflict, sparked by imperial and dynastic interests. Europe's soldiers locked horns not only on the continental mainland but also far overseas, in theaters very different to the woods and fields of their homelands.

The causes of the Seven Years' War, as with so many 18th-century conflicts, are difficult to detail. The seeds were sown in clashes between Austria-Hungary and Prussia over possession of the province of Silesia, but the conflict expanded dramatically as European alliances formed broader opposing sides. Ultimately, an alliance of Austria, France, Russia, Sweden, and Saxony fought against Britain, Prussia, and Hanover, each power bringing its own vested interests.

Frederick the Great

Frederick II of Prussia (1712–86) was arguably the greatest of the commanders of the Seven Years' War. A highly cultured man, he was also a superb military theorist and a personally courageous soldier.

▲ Frederick the Great is hailed by men of the Bernburg Regiment after the Battle at Liegnitz, 1760.

◀ The British commander General Edward Braddock meets his end near Fort Duquesne, Ohio Country, in 1755, during the French and Indian War in North America.

"The **most exact discipline** is ever to be maintained, **and the greatest regard** paid to their [soldiers'] welfare."

FREDERICK THE GREAT, IN 1750

WIDESPREAD WAR

What we broadly label the Seven Years' War can rather more accurately be regarded as several major related conflicts coexisting at different locations across the world. Over mainland Europe, the center of the clash was between France/Austria and Prussia/Britain, involving huge set-piece engagements at places such as Rossbach, Leuthen, and Minden, but the fighting stretched well beyond Europe, as the warring nations also clashed in their overseas colonies.

Fighting was especially heavy in North America, with France and Britain both struggling to achieve dominance in what is today Canada and the United States. A unique dimension was added to this conflict (known as the French and Indian War) by the fact that both sides struck alliances with Native American tribes, mixing native skills in "irregular" warfare with the European ranks in disciplined battlefield formations.

Far away from the Americas, the war also touched Africa and Asia. In West Africa, a British military expedition in 1758 attacked and captured the French settlement of Saint-Louis in Senegal. The French and British also fought over their trading colonies in India, bringing local Indian armies into the conflict. Other theaters of war included

▲ Friedrich Wilhelm von Seydlitz was an exceptional Prussian cavalry commander, who led with distinction during the Seven Years' War.

the Mediterranean, Philippines, and Caribbean. The big winners in the conflict were Britain and Prussia; France and Austria suffered major defeats.

ARMIES

The soldiers of the Seven Years' War, as the geographical picture indicates, were a mixed bunch, from tomahawk-wielding Native Americans to European-trained Indian infantry. By this time, however, most European powers had some form of standing army —a permanent, largely full-time force employed by the state—supplemented by plentiful supplies of mercenaries, of variable quality and commitment.

◄ A Prussian military officer is looted by Cossacks after the Battle of Kunersdorf, 1759, the scene of Frederick the Great's heaviest defeat during the conflict.

THE EUROPEAN ARMIES

The Seven Years' War, like all major conflicts, placed a strain on existing military manpower. Armies had to rapidly recruit, train, and deploy soldiers in huge numbers, and also maintain their pay and living conditions while in the field.

Recruiting soldiers was a problem for even the most competent of the European armies during the Seven Years' War. Russia had the greatest volume of manpower, with a total force of 333,000 men. Yet the quality of this army left a lot to be desired. Only about 174,000 men were actually first-line soldiers; the rest were poorly trained and (usually) apathetically led militia and garrison troops. Hence Russia typically committed only about 60,000–90,000 men to a campaign at any one time.

▲ A Prussian Army camp around the time of the Seven Years' War. Large numbers of canvas tents were carried in the supply train.

PROFESSIONALISM

The picture across the other European armies showed generally smaller armies, with varying degrees of professionalism. Prussia had a highly skilled force of 145,000 men at the beginning of the war, in which soldiers were recruited on a district basis, thus maintaining local loyalties. Following recruitment, the individual Prussian soldier served with either a regular field regiment or a garrison regiment (during wartime the latter served as a reserve for the former). Training standards were high, especially in precision battlefield maneuvers and the handling of weaponry. However, like many nations, Prussia could not afford to strip its agricultural sector of valuable manpower all year round. Therefore, regular soldiers would often return to their family fields outside campaign season, undergoing refresher training when they were called up again the following year.

PRISONERS AND DESERTERS

The district recruitment system worked well in peacetime, but was stretched to breaking point during the war. For this reason, Prussia was compelled to

◄ The Battle of Minden on August 1, 1759, saw French troops defeated, with 7,000 losses, by an Anglo-German alliance, which lost fewer than 3,000 men.

BRITISH GRENADIER, 1756

Grenadiers, as their name suggests, had the job of throwing grenades during an assault. In the 18th century British grenadiers were distinguished by their tall miter caps, which displayed regimental information.

Firearm
The soldier is armed with the Long Land Pattern "Brown Bess" musket.

Coat
Most British regiments (apart from artillery) wore red coats with regimental facing colors.

Mitasses
The long leggings were especially useful when fighting in woodland terrain.

> "The **strictest care** and the most **unremitting attention are required** of commanding officers in the **formation of my troops**."
>
> FREDERICK THE GREAT, c. 1750

accept large numbers of mercenaries, who constituted up to 25 percent of the entire army in 1756. Later, it also had to drag in enemy deserters and prisoners to fill out the ranks.

These practices were not unusual. Britain had a small army of 90,000 in 1756, with many men deployed to the colonies. To flesh out the ranks, recruiters often combed civilian prisons, offering desperate men release in return for military service. Other men were even press-ganged into uniform, having been plied with liquor—waking from their hangover in a military barracks.

The French Army, though sizable at 200,000 men, suffered from very low morale and discipline. Desertion and alcoholism became endemic problems, contributing to the French defeat.

▼ Eighteenth-century drill instruction seems formulaic today, but at the time was essential for coordinated movement and fire on the battlefield.

LIFE IN THE CAVALRY

The cavalry were the shock troops of the battlefield. Although viewed historically as somewhat glamorous and dashing compared to the humble infantry, they still shared in the hardships of the campaign, and fulfilled many mundane duties.

The cavalry forces of the Seven Years' War had an obvious part to play in battlefield tactics. Their mobility meant they were suited not only to direct, bludgeoning charges against the enemy, but also to sudden attacks against exposed flanks and the pursuit of a routed enemy. They also offered a protective service to the shuffling infantry, providing defensive and offensive reconnaissance, and shielding foraging parties.

THE PRUSSIAN CAVALRYMAN

Each army had its own cavalry traditions and tactics, although a degree of conformity means that we can here usefully explore the cavalry of just one army, that of Prussia.

The Prussian cavalry became one of the most reliable elements of Frederick's army, and the least prone to desertion. Partly this was to do with the high standards of recruiting. Most of the heavy cavalry (dragoons and

▲ British carabineers make the charge at the Battle of Warburg, July 31, 1760, making forehand and backhand cuts with their sabers.

▼ Cavalry were most vulnerable to musket and artillery fire, the horse making a large and convenient target for even the most inaccurate or inexperienced musketeer.

cuirassiers), for example, were from free peasant stock, bringing with them a physical toughness and a genuine loyalty and affection for their mounts, as well as experience in looking after them. Training was excellent—typically two years of cavalry instruction, including individual horsemanship and large-scale tactical maneuvers.

EYEWITNESS ACCOUNT

"When an officer has made his patrole...he may allow half of his party to go into the nearest peasants' houses, unsaddle, unbridle, and feed half of the horses, and...suffer the remaining half to do the same. But if the enemy be in the neighborhood... he must remain hid in the rear of the village, and feed his horses tied to a hedge."
—Frederick the Great, 1797

> "The enemy **began a heavy fire upon the cavalry**, which brought them to a stand, and obliged them **to desist**."

COL. TEMPELHOFFE, ON THE BATTLE OF KOLIN, 1757

▲ A French recruitment poster calls for men to join the dragoons, a type of mounted infantry who could fight on foot or from horseback.

SIZING UP

One noticeable distinction between Prussian heavy and light cavalrymen was their physical size. Heavy cavalrymen, being given the largest horses, had to have a minimum height of 5 ft 5 in/1.65 m, while the same height requirement was the maximum allowed for the fleet-footed hussars.

All cavalrymen had to perform daily duties of care for their horses and equipment. Frederick noted: "Minute attention must be paid by the general that the cavalry officers repair their saddles, bridles, stirrups, and boots." Frederick gave this advice from practical experience. A broken saddle strap or defective stirrup could result in a cavalryman being thrown during combat. The cavalryman was also responsible for inspecting his horse for minor wounds or defective shoes.

PRUSSIAN HUSSAR, 1756
Hussars became a far larger and more influential force under Frederick II than they had been before his ascension. A hussar had to demonstrate complete dexterity and accuracy with his chief weapon, the light saber.

Pelisse
The short, tailless pelisse jacket was classically worn over the left shoulder.

Saber
The saber had a fine point, curved blade and an iron stirrup hilt.

Boots
The Prussian Hussars wore Hungarian-style cavalry boots.

THE INFANTRY'S EXPERIENCE

The life of an infantryman in any army during this time was one of hardship and toil, with few creature comforts. Remuneration was also poor, and the chances of promotion limited by external circumstances.

The 18th-century British soldier is a useful representative for a closer examination of the life of the 18th-century infantryman. Recruits for the infantry tended to be drawn from the poorest sectors of society—the desire to escape poverty was a powerful motivation behind armed service —principally from young (teenage) unmarried men. Often the recruiters would acquire such men at hiring fairs, if the young men struggled to find work in the civilian market. To join the infantry, men had to be at least 5 ft 6 in/ 1.67 m tall, reasonably fit, Protestant (in Britain at this time, Catholics were prohibited from service) and without an egregious criminal record. Once accepted into the ranks, the recruit took the "King's shilling."

▼ British infantry troops scale the Heights of Abraham during the critical battle just outside Quebec City, fought on September 13, 1759.

GRENADIER, HESSEN-DARMSTADT LEIB GRENADIERS, 1759
Grenadiers were often given the most dangerous roles on the battlefield, and were regarded in many armies as something of an elite.

Cartridge box
The leather pouch contains paper cartridges, each holding powder and ball.

Musket
Maximum rate of fire for a smoothbore musket was about 3 rounds per minute (rpm).

Gaiters
White cloth gaiters were secured by a row of buttons on the outer side.

> ### "...the **Files must be so close**, that the Men **almost touch one another** with their Shoulders."
>
> HUMPHREY BLAND, *TREATISE OF MILITARY DISCIPLINE*, 1762

PAY AND CONDITIONS

The basic wage for a private soldier was 8 pence per day, minus deductions for uniform and subsistence. On promotion to sergeant, the soldier would be paid the princely sum of 1 shilling and 6 pence per day. By the time deductions had been made, however, there would be little hard cash in his pocket.

Once posted to a regiment, the soldier would live either in a typically overcrowded barrack, or be billeted in civilian accommodation, such as an inn or outbuilding. Note that the soldier was by no means destined to serve in just one regiment for life; he might be posted to several regiments over the course of a long military career, if not cut short by death or disability.

MAKING A SOLDIER

Training for the new soldier varied considerably; the man might find himself sent to an operational unit in the New World with scarcely more than a few weeks of instruction. Training would continue within his unit, however, and after about a year he would be considered a proficient soldier. It was possible for a soldier who showed dependability and bravery to rise through the noncommissioned officer (NCO) ranks, and take a commission, but it remained difficult for "rankers" to become officers in the 18th century. Service for many men was technically lifelong, but administrative realities meant this was rare.

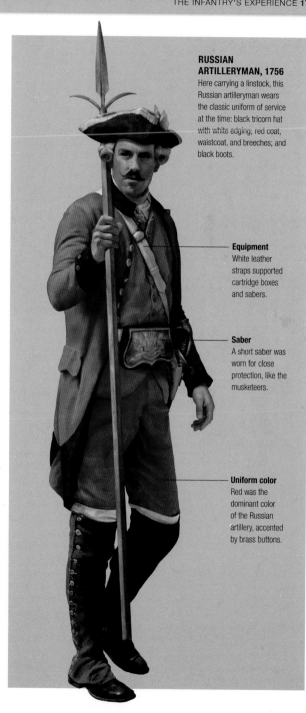

RUSSIAN ARTILLERYMAN, 1756
Here carrying a linstock, this Russian artilleryman wears the classic uniform of service at the time: black tricorn hat with white edging; red coat, waistcoat, and breeches; and black boots.

Equipment
White leather straps supported cartridge boxes and sabers.

Saber
A short saber was worn for close protection, like the musketeers.

Uniform color
Red was the dominant color of the Russian artillery, accented by brass buttons.

BATTLEFIELD FORMATIONS

During the 17th century, European armies experimented with ways in which they could maximize the effect of their musket power. By the Seven Years' War, soldiers on the battlefield had to perform maneuvers of near-clockwork precision.

In an age of inaccurate personal weaponry (a musket had an effective range of only around 110 yards/100 m), commanders had to develop set battlefield positions to compensate. The two formations that infantry had to master during the Seven Years' War were the column and the line.

RANKED FIRE

The end goal of battlefield infantry formations was to outmaneuver the enemy and to bring a long line of firepower to bear on his ranks as quickly as possible. By massing the infantry in a linear fashion, shoulder to shoulder, and coordinating their musket fire, the mass of firepower compensated for the individual inaccuracies of the muskets. One of the quickest ways to move into a ranked line was by marching the troops into position in a

▲ The success of battlefield formations required clear commands from an officer, although these were easily lost in the din of battle.

▼ British troops on the morning of the Battle of the Plains of Abraham, ordered in ranks ready to take firing, assault, or defensive positions.

narrow column, then making a simple quarter turn to present the muskets toward the enemy.

The infantry would be arrayed in two or three ranks—three was often regarded as the ideal, but manpower issues or tactical choice frequently reduced these to two. To complicate matters, a battalion of infantry was often subdivided into discrete firing units (or platoons). So the commanders and the men would have to coordinate their fire and reloading sequences through the depth of the ranks and across the platoon frontage: no easy matter in the noise and chaos of battle.

> "Discipline is the soul of an army. It makes small numbers formidable; procures success to the weak, and esteem to all."
> GEORGE WASHINGTON, 1759

MOVEMENT

Terrain would have a big effect on the movement of soldiers around a battlefield. Trees, bushes, swampy ground, ravines, streams, or any other natural feature could break up a line formation, potentially exposing breaks that could be exploited by an enemy cavalry or an infantry assault. Also, if the line had to perform any sort of pivoting movement, the soldiers on the outer arm of the pivot had to move more quickly than those at the "hinge."

SHARED DANGERS

The human experience of fighting from these serried ranks could be unnerving. The soldiers would be standing shoulder to shoulder. If someone was killed or wounded, the men on either side would witness that event at harrowingly close quarters. Indeed, sometimes soldiers were injured by the bone fragments of nearby men blown apart by cannon shot. The environment would have been smoky and loud, with muzzle flashes and reports next to the faces of those in the front ranks.

▶ Attack formations moved forward in line then made the assault in line or in a staggered wave. The wave needed more control but was less vulnerable to gunfire.

▼ The Siege of Pondicherry, India, 1760. Artillery placement was a critical command decision, the guns needing clear fields of fire through friendly troops.

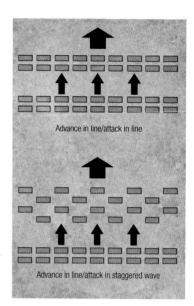

Advance in line/attack in line

Advance in line/attack in staggered wave

FACETS OF WAR: MIND AND MORALE

Despite centuries of warfare, military psychology is only a recently accepted phenomenon, a study born of the late 19th century. This has produced a deeper understanding of how to keep soldiers mentally functioning on the battlefield and long after.

There has always been an awareness that soldiering, and the experience of combat, can be hard on the mind. The so-called Lewis chess set, a 12th-century chess set discovered in the Outer Hebrides in 1831, includes figures of 'berserkers' ready for battle, literally chewing on the top of their shields with the sheer mental tension of hand-to-hand combat.

Scroll forward to our modern age, and we now have an extremely detailed picture of the potential psychological effects of witnessing or participating in military violence, from the occasional nightmare through to the crippling post-traumatic stress disorder (PTSD). So do we now understand what makes a soldier crumble, or cope, under pressure?

▲ Officers of the 114th Pennsylvania Infantry relax in camp during the Civil War. Leisure time has always been critical to restoring a soldier's mental health.

► Kaiser Wilhelm II reviews his troops. Morale is closely tied to good leadership—soldiers must have confidence in command decisions to believe in their objectives.

become accustomed to the perennial hunger of life on campaign. Today, conditioning is meted out through intense physical fitness challenges plus ultrarealistic combat training using nonlethal ammunition and high-pressure tactical scenarios.

R & R

No matter how well conditioned the soldier, prolonged exposure to a mix of combat and fatigue will eventually produce psychological breakdown. This is why "rest and recuperation" (R & R) is central to modern mind management. Studies from World War II showed that soldiers could endure a maximum of 14 days of combat before they needed to be pulled out to a safe rear area for sleep and readjustment. Base life also had to support mental restoration—music, contact with home and family, sport, clean uniform, good food, and, above all, sleep, will all have a profound effect on a soldier's well-being. In many ways, it is easy to tell a professional army from a poor army by the investment it makes in the mental side of soldiering.

BATTLE INOCULATION

A key ingredient of effective mental conditioning for a soldier lies in the nature of his or her training. The more realistic and dangerous the training, the better the soldier becomes acclimatized to the adrenaline rush and shock of battle, and is less likely to collapse mentally when faced with real combat. Many armies have understood this even in times before modern psychology formalized it. Back in ancient Sparta, for example, the preparatory *agoge* program included constant pain conditioning for the young would-be warriors; it also deprived them of sufficient food so that they would

▲ An American military theatrical group, in the early 20th century. Given the physical isolation of many deployments, soldiers produce their own forms of entertainment.

▼ A U.S. soldier picks out a tune on his guitar. Soldiers often report how certain individuals are central to the well-being of a unit, supporting others and raising morale.

▼ Contact with family provides the soldier with continuity through the disruption of war. Here American troops line up for a pay phone call during their basic training.

THE OFFICER CLASS

Frequently, although not always, high born, the officer class in the Seven Years' War had every shade and hue of competence and experience. Much depended on the personal qualities of the leader as to whether his unit would thrive or fail.

It was the nobility and the gentry who formed either a majority or a very high percentage of the officer class in all the European armies during the Seven Years' War. A list of senior officers from Prussian army records just prior to the conflict showed that 34 officers of general rank were all noblemen, and only 11 of 211 field officers came from what we would now term the middle classes.

CHANGING COMPOSITION

War has a way of changing social patterns, and the officer class was especially vulnerable. Unlike in our modern age, the senior officers of the past tended to lead from the front, putting themselves within range of musket ball and cannon shot, hence their losses were extremely heavy. In the Prussian forces, Frederick the Great was compelled to accept more bourgeois commissions from

▶ A wounded officer is carried off the battlefield by his men, whether through loyalty or just sheer obedience is unclear.

> "...**Lieutenant-Colonel fell killed**...beyond this we lost our Major, and indeed **all the Officers but three.**"
>
> AUSTRIAN EYEWITNESS, LEUTHEN, 1757

▼ Frederick the Great leads his soldiers at the Battle of Zorndorf, 1758, defeating the Russians although his own army suffered 11,000 casualties.

experienced troops to fill out the ranks. The Apenburg Dragoons, for example, had no bourgeois officers at the beginning of the war, but five (out of 37) by the end of the war. Britain, by contrast, had just 40 percent of its total officers from noble stock, the rest ascending largely through merit. What was consistent across national armies was that officer training was

EYEWITNESS ACCOUNT

"The field you are going into is quite new to you, but may be trod very safely... Your character in life must be that of a soldier and a gentleman; the first is to be acquired by application and attendance to your duty; the second by adhering most strictly to the dictates of honor, and the rules of good breeding; and be most particular in each of these points when you join your Regiment."
—Lieutenant-Colonel James Wolfe, advice to a young officer, 1756

▲ Major-General James Wolfe was one of Britain's finest officers, a man not afraid to experiment with both battlefield tactics and technology.

generally poor. Based on the belief that noble officers brought with them superior intelligence and moral fiber, "training" was largely confined to "on the job" experience and the advice of more senior and experienced officers. This being said, some unit commanders made efforts to ensure that their junior officers underwent a formal period of tutelage to grasp the fundamentals of drill, tactics, and combat technology.

MONEY MATTERS

Being an officer was a very expensive business. Officers were expected to set themselves apart from the other ranks in every aspect of their presentation, social life, and accommodation. Particular financial drains included the cost of maintaining a horse, food and drink at the officers' mess, and interest on loans. It was perfectly common, therefore, for a less moneyed officer to fall into financial hardship, as outgoings matched or exceeded incomings.

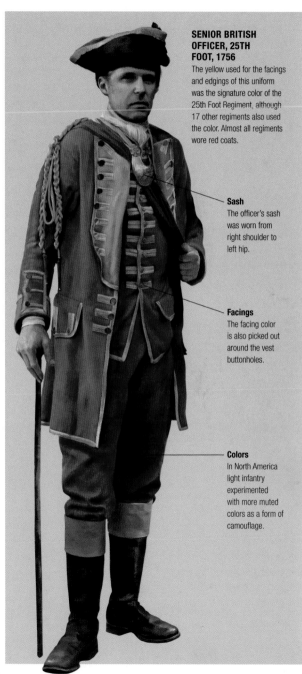

SENIOR BRITISH OFFICER, 25TH FOOT, 1756

The yellow used for the facings and edgings of this uniform was the signature color of the 25th Foot Regiment, although 17 other regiments also used the color. Almost all regiments wore red coats.

Sash
The officer's sash was worn from right shoulder to left hip.

Facings
The facing color is also picked out around the vest buttonholes.

Colors
In North America light infantry experimented with more muted colors as a form of camouflage.

ON THE MOVE

Getting an army from one place to another was no easy business in the 18th century. Operational movement for the vast majority of soldiers was performed the hard way—on foot—with horses and mules providing the muscle for logistics.

In principle, getting an army to march from one place to another seems simple enough. In practice, and not least in the context of the Seven Years' War, such movements were taxing at both human and administrative levels.

PHYSICAL ORDEAL
Even for physically hardened soldiers, long repeated campaign marches were a punishing business. Knee and ankle joints would swell up and become

▶ British troops in the French and Indian War produce crude improvised log footbridges to cross a ravine.

▼ Highlanders talk with Native American warriors. During the French and Indian War, the British began training their light infantry in Native American-style irregular warfare techniques of movement.

extremely painful. Leather straps could rub skin raw, requiring constant improvised padding. Uniforms would become caked in filth and riddled with lice. Shoes and boots might be holed in a matter of days, keeping regimental cobblers busy.

The two key factors were terrain and distance. Regarding distance, an expected rate of march in Frederick the Great's army was 15 miles/24 km a day. In reality, this rate could not be sustained indefinitely, on account of soldier and horse fatigue and the distance from supply depots. The nature of the terrain was also critical. In the French and Indian War especially,

> "We must **gain a knowledge of the roads** ...to be satisfied in **how many columns we may march**."
>
> FREDERICK THE GREAT, C. 1750

troops were confronted with the North American wilderness in all its obdurate glory. In 1755, during General Braddock's expedition against the French, British troops took 18 hours to travel through 3 miles/5 km of particularly difficult terrain.

RATIONS AND LOGISTICS

For logisticians, a marching army involved daunting calculations regarding rations. Soldiers on the move require more rations than soldiers conserving calories in barracks, so logisticians had to ensure that the soldiers had enough food to sustain them through the journey. For Frederick the Great's campaign in Saxony in 1756, for example, it was calculated that his army would need a total daily consumption of 76,235 individual ration portions.

The rations also had to be durable, as far as possible. Bread was the main

▲ British hussars move through a North American village. Cavalry would try to operate within a day's ride of forage depots.

◄ When the march stopped, carpenters got to work building accommodation. These traditional carpentry tools are: 1 wood saw; 2 hammer; 3 wood compass; 4 gimlet; 5 wire snips; 6 wood plane; 7 folding ruler; 8 portable hammer and anvil set.

food carried by soldiers on campaign, but after a day it would be stale and within two or three days it would turn moldy. (The bread would be carried in nothing more than a cloth bag, possibly wrapped in paper.) A campaign march, therefore, would be accompanied by field bakeries, which would produce fresh loaves almost every day. Field bakeries also needed to be supported by intensive logistics—in the Prussian campaign, for example, 400 horse wagons were dedicated solely to transporting the ingredients and equipment for the field bakeries.

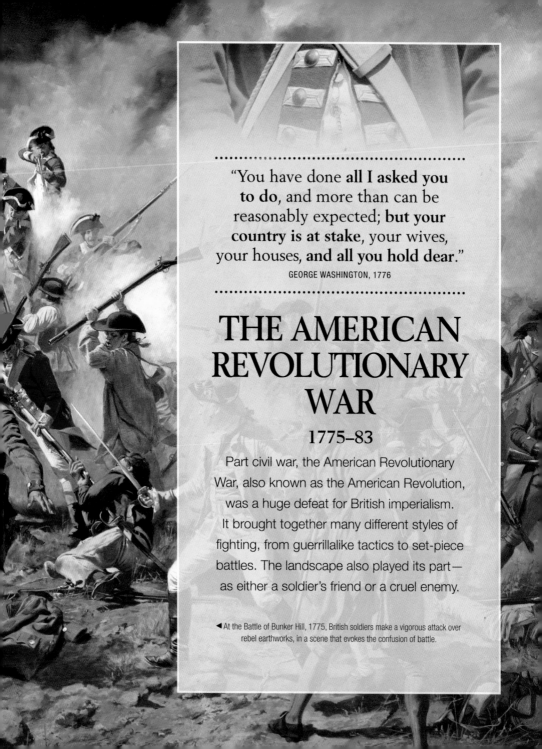

> "You have done **all I asked you to do**, and more than can be reasonably expected; **but your country is at stake**, your wives, your houses, **and all you hold dear.**"
>
> GEORGE WASHINGTON, 1776

THE AMERICAN REVOLUTIONARY WAR

1775–83

Part civil war, the American Revolutionary War, also known as the American Revolution, was a huge defeat for British imperialism. It brought together many different styles of fighting, from guerrillalike tactics to set-piece battles. The landscape also played its part— as either a soldier's friend or a cruel enemy.

◀ At the Battle of Bunker Hill, 1775, British soldiers make a vigorous attack over rebel earthworks, in a scene that evokes the confusion of battle.

A NATIONAL UPRISING

The American Revolutionary War changed the face of global politics, and its principles still resonate around the world today. It demonstrated how the coordinated efforts of a resistant people could defeat even the world's greatest imperial power.

The bare historical bones of the Revolutionary War are well known to most high-school students. In 1773, citizens of Boston destroyed a large consignment of British-imported tea in the city harbor, as part of a developing popular protest against British taxation and the lack of any American representation in the British government. Britain's efforts to quash the growing rebellion failed, and the early sparks were fanned into a continental war, with American independence as the colonists' ultimate prize. Eight bloody years later, they achieved their goal with the final defeat of British forces at Yorktown. The loss was a shattering blow to British prestige and confidence.

▶ The Declaration of Independence, adopted on July 4, 1776, is in essence the birth certificate of the United States of America.

....

"We **formed, advanced,** and **fired upon the enemy**... Their ranks grew thin and **victory seemed complete.**"

US CONTINENTAL ARMY SERGEANT, 1777

....

▼ The Boston Massacre (1770), when British redcoats fired into a crowd and killed five civilian men. Such incidents fueled the independence movement.

MISPERCEPTIONS

From a military point of view, the Revolutionary War is often misrepresented, or at least heavily simplified. For example, it is often depicted as a clash between wily rebels using free-spirited guerrilla tactics to defeat straight-backed ranks of tradition-bound British troops. This image has an element of truth, as we shall see, but the picture is far more complicated, especially as George Washington's Continental Army grew into a sizable, structured force, capable of conducting major set-piece battles.

We must also remember—a fact often downplayed in popular histories—that the French were a significant presence on the side of the Americans. At the Battle of Yorktown, for example, the Americans mustered 8,845 men onto the field of battle, but they were supported by no fewer than 7,800

French troops, almost the same number as the British who opposed them.

CIVIL CONFLICT

Another important point of understanding regarding the Revolutionary War is that it was partly

▲ George Washington (on horseback) witnesses the death of comrade General Hugh Mercer at the Battle of Princeton, 1777.

▼ Tombstones from the revolutionary era in a cemetery in Boston, a key battleground.

a civil war. Not all the colonists were eager to break ties with Britain, and many thousands fought as loyalists, either under British command or by creating independent units. The eventual outcome of the war was therefore felt as a defeat rather than a victory for many Americans.

The Revolutionary War is a fascinating conflict from a military and social historian's point of view. Because the conflict was in essence a "people's war," involving a broad spectrum of society, we see all manner of individuals in uniform (and all manner of uniforms, for that matter). At one end of the scale were some truly amateurish local militia units, poorly armed and badly led, but still a thorn in the side of the British. At the other end we have the British Army—skilled, professional soldiers who were nevertheless destined for defeat.

MILITIAS AND THE MINUTEMEN

When the Revolutionary War began in 1775, the rebel forces were a rough-and-ready mix of part-time militia forces. Although derided by some, including George Washington, the militias nonetheless fought some vital actions in the early years of the war.

The tradition of creating and maintaining militias—part-time citizen forces called into action on a needs basis—went back to the earliest days of American colonization, when groups of men were formed to provide communities with local defense against Native American tribes and foreign invasion. With the outbreak of war in 1775, these were essentially the only troops that the American rebel commanders had at their disposal.

CITIZEN SOLDIERS

The militia troops were configured for short-term threats, not long-term conflicts. Many of them were agricultural workers, subsistence farmers or low-level businessmen, who had to return home to their work on a regular, often seasonal, basis. This caused a range of problems for the early American war effort, resulting in troop deficits at key moments. The issue contributed, in the prewar years, to the designation of certain proportions of

▲ Revolutionary troops occupy defensive positions, waiting for a British attack in 1775.

▼ Minutemen live up to their name, and are mustered at short notice to face the British, April 19, 1775.

militia troops as "minutemen." These were individuals who could mobilize to meet threats at any time of the year, almost immediately—with a minute's notice. They were young, unmarried, and demonstrated skill with a gun.

EYEWITNESS ACCOUNT

"When I arrived there, I inquired of Captain Parker, the commander of the Lexington company, what was the news... But while we were talking, a messenger came up and told the captain that the British troops were within half a mile. Parker immediately turned to his drummer, William Diman, and ordered him to beat to arms, which was done."
—Sylvanus Wood, 1775

MINUTEMAN, CULPEPER COUNTY, 1775

The minutemen of Culpeper County, Virginia, were formed on July 17, 1775. By the fall of that year, their strength had risen to around 250 men.

Motto
"Liberty or Death" was an official motto of the Culpeper minutemen.

Powder horn
The powder horn held about 1 pound/0.45 kg of gunpowder.

Leggings
The woollen leggings were wrapped around the leg and tied at the knee.

RAG-TAG ARMY

The American militias were generally not polished or professional units, at any level of their ranks. The initial criteria for service, laid down by the Continental Congress on July 18, 1775, were based on supplies. Any man could present himself for service if he brought with him a decent musket, bayonet, sword, or tomahawk, a cartridge box containing 24 rounds of ammunition, plus 2.2 pounds/ 0.9 kg of gunpowder and the same weight of lead (to make into musketballs), and a knapsack to keep it all in. There was no regulation uniform, consistent leadership, training, or discipline, and the militia troops often struggled to hold their own against the well-drilled British forces.

Yet many militiamen brought with them experience of irregular warfare against the Native Americans, together with a hardened knowledge of how to live off the land and move through it with ease. This combination of skills was vital, and meant that, while the militias were susceptible to defeat in open battle, they still made a valuable contribution to the final outcome.

▼ Militia troops often lacked all semblance of uniformity, although from 1776–77 many units began to wear more standardized elements of military uniform.

THE CONTINENTAL ARMY

Washington's Continental Army was America's first attempt at establishing its own standing army. It began as a volatile force of unpredictable quality and commitment, yet it ultimately managed to take on and defeat the British, even in open warfare.

The decision to form a permanent standing army was an inevitable one for Congress. Although the militia troops could chip away at British resolve, what was required was a professional, well-trained army that could confront and defeat the enemy in open battle.

COHESION AND COMMITMENT

The act of establishment was taken on June 14, 1775, with George Washington as its commander. The soldiers who made up the Continental Army in those

▼ Continental Army artillery and cavalry seen here on the march. The artillery often used captured British guns as much as indigenously produced pieces.

early years were drawn from across the 13 colonial states. They were a motley bunch, and included (to make up the numbers) former deserters, freed slaves, "turned" British prisoners of war, ex-convicts, and mercenaries. They were enlisted to serve for three years or the duration of the war, but maintaining this long-term commitment was a huge problem, compounded by endless difficulties with paying and supplying the troops. At times the soldiers lived in a state of fairly extreme deprivation, short of even the most basic supplies of food and items of clothing, to say nothing of arms and ammunition.

INFANTRY RATION

Official rations of a Continental Army infantryman in 1775 were: 1 pound/450 g of beef or salt fish and 1 pound/450 g of bread a day; 3 pints/1.4 liters of peas or beans a week; 1 pint/475 ml of milk a day; ½ pint/240 ml of rice a week; 2 pints/1 liter of beer or cider a day. Campaign conditions would reduce rations significantly.

▲ A Continental Army color guard, playing fife and drum (primary means of battlefield communication in the 18th century), lead a formation of infantry onward through winter conditions.

TRAINING

Until 1778, levels of discipline and training among the Continental Army soldiers were generally low. Most men brought only the training they had received in the militias—typically about one day per week, plus an annual regimental exercise. In 1778, however, the Prussian mercenary General Baron Friedrich Wilhelm von Steuben began serious efforts to both raise the quality of training and standardize it throughout the ranks by producing general training manuals. The individual rank and file might not read the manuals, but their commanders were likely to, so the knowledge would trickle down through the ranks.

· ·

"The unfortunate soldiers **were in want of everything**; they had **neither coats nor hats, nor shirts nor shoes.**"

CLAUDE BLANCHARD, 1780

· ·

PRIVATE, HALL'S DELAWARE REGIMENT, 1780
The Delaware Regiment was formed in December 1775. In 1779, Washington implemented a general order that defined uniform facing colors to distinguish the state origins of regiments— Delaware's color was red.

Water canteen
Made of lacquered wood, when full the canteen weighed about 2 pounds/0.9 kg.

Ration bag
A day's rations would be held in a simple cloth bag.

Musket
The musket weighed around 10 pounds/4.5 kg.

BRITISH AND LOYALIST FORCES

Representing the Revolutionary War as "Americans vs. British" is misleading. Fighting alongside the British were considerable numbers of American loyalists, whose local knowledge proved invaluable to the overseas troops.

The British Army was undoubtedly a force to be respected by even the most hardy of rebels. The British "redcoat" often hailed from some of the most deprived sectors of society, but as a long-serving regular he would be molded into a toughened professional. In fact, most British soldiers in America brought with them 5–15 years of prior service, and those who joined up during the war would have received at least six months of basic training.

ON THE BACK FOOT

The British soldiers in North America quickly realized that the war was about more than just face-to-face confrontations with the enemy. The distances involved in North America stretched their logistics to and often beyond breaking point, especially as many of their supplies were shipped in via troubled transatlantic supply routes. Hunger and worn uniforms became hallmarks of the British experience. A classic dish when times were good

▼ The rebel heroine Nancy Hart takes a group of British troops captive in a famous episode that embodies the friction between British troops and American civilians.

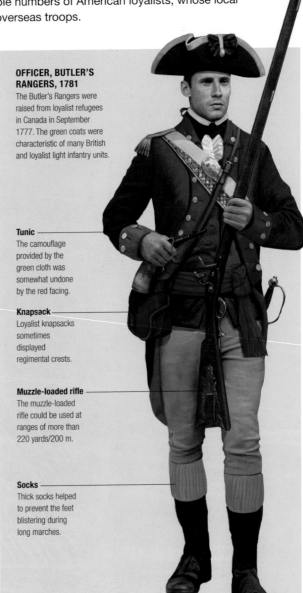

OFFICER, BUTLER'S RANGERS, 1781
The Butler's Rangers were raised from loyalist refugees in Canada in September 1777. The green coats were characteristic of many British and loyalist light infantry units.

Tunic
The camouflage provided by the green cloth was somewhat undone by the red facing.

Knapsack
Loyalist knapsacks sometimes displayed regimental crests.

Muzzle-loaded rifle
The muzzle-loaded rifle could be used at ranges of more than 220 yards/200 m.

Socks
Thick socks helped to prevent the feet blistering during long marches.

GRENADIER, 17TH FOOT, 1777

This British soldier wears the familiar red coat. Note that through experience British soldiers might cut short the tails of their coats, to prevent them snagging on undergrowth.

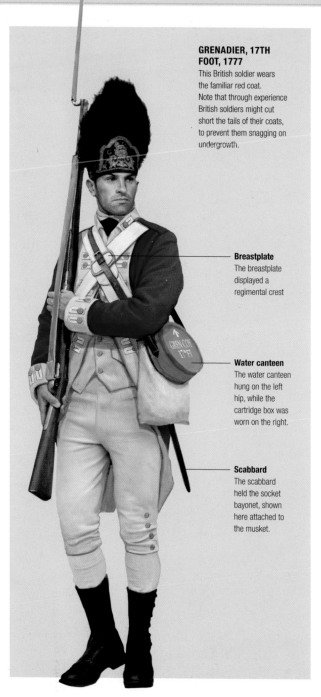

Breastplate
The breastplate displayed a regimental crest

Water canteen
The water canteen hung on the left hip, while the cartridge box was worn on the right.

Scabbard
The scabbard held the socket bayonet, shown here attached to the musket.

▲ Although the British technically won the Battle of Guilford Courthouse in 1781, they lost so many men that their subsequent advance into Virginia was doomed.

was beef broth and potatoes, washed down with "small beer," a weak brew that was safer than water—the brewing process killed off most harmful bacteria. On campaign, the diet was less hearty, the troops living off what the woodland or a looted farm provided.

FIGHTING FOR THE CAUSE

The British were supported in the war by a broad spectrum of other warriors. Many Native Americans fought under British alliances, and some 30 percent of the British troops were actually German—"Hessian"—mercenaries who displayed talent in light infantry warfare. There were also large numbers of American "loyalist" troops. It is hard to generalize about the loyalist soldier. Some formed prestigious conventional regiments, such as the King's Royal Regiment, Queen's Regiment, and Butler's Rangers, while others were used as light skirmishers or merely as security or garrison troops. Some were therefore dressed in formal military livery, while others might be in the rough garb of a backwoodsman.

The loyalists fought with varied motives, perhaps from a sense of loyalty to the homeland, or strong commercial or family ties across the Atlantic.

IRREGULAR WARFARE

Although the general use of guerrilla tactics can be overstated in the context of the American Revolutionary War, it is certainly the case that unconventional warfare was used by the rebels to inflict attrition on their foes.

Although the vast bulk of the rebel forces consisted of regular line infantry, Washington's army also included light infantry troops, riflemen, and groups of independent-minded "rangers." These were no mere skirmishers. Able to take accurate long-range shots with a muzzle-loading rifle, many of these troops were also experts in conducting scouting missions deep into enemy territory, blending into the land to evade British detection.

MARKSMEN

The defining firearm of the American rifleman was a muzzle-loading rifle. This weapon had a barrel several feet long, frequently longer than the barrel

► The lock mechanism was the most temperamental part of a rifleman's weapon. The flint had to be accurately shaped to strike a spark consistently from the steel.

▼ Musketry tools and equipment. 1 mainspring vice; 2 ball puller; 3 tompion; 4 and 5 flint and striker; 6 pick and pan brush; 7 pickering tool; 8 musket tool; 9 steel wool; 10 scraper; 11 flint hammer; 12 bore brush; 13 wooden flint; 14 spare flint; 15 jag tool; 16 worm tool; 17 ramrod/tool adapter; 18 powder measure.

of a conventional smoothbore musket. The length of the barrel delivered a high muzzle velocity, while the rifling imparted a stabilizing gyroscopic spin to the musket ball, qualities that made the rifle more accurate over distance. The result was that American riflemen could take out individual targets (ideally British officers) from positions of cover at ranges of more than 300 yards/275 m. Dressed in early types of camouflage and with knowledge of the terrain, they could also blend back into the landscape after taking the shot.

LIVING LIGHT

In addition to marksmanship, many American light infantry and rangers also possessed true survival skills. It should be noted that the British also operated ranger units and employed professional scouts, so the skills described here were not exclusive to the rebels. They

▲ A light infantryman takes aim with his muzzle-loading rifle; the man behind and to his right has just rammed down powder, ball, and paper.

> "When you **return from a scout**, and come near our forts, **avoid the usual roads...**"
>
> ROBERT ROGERS, FROM THE 28 "RULES OF RANGING," 1757

basic rations, musketry kit, dagger and tomahawk, seasonal clothing (including buckskin breeches, hunting shirts, and moccasins), cooking and eating utensils, and a knapsack for rations. An article in the *Pennsylvania Journal* from 1775 sums up the men's qualities: "These men have been bred in the woods to hardships and dangers since their infancy. They appear as if they were entirely unacquainted with, and had never felt, the passion of fear."

▼ Ranger scouts, lightly dressed in hunting clothing, check a campfire to see how long it has been since the occupants of the camp were present.

could navigate rivers in basic birchbark canoes or whaleboats made from cedar planking. They could build campfires in even the most inclement conditions, and a "shed" shelter of branches and bark would take an experienced soldier about 30 minutes to erect. In winter, the soldiers would construct their shelters using more insulating pine boughs, angling the mouths of the shelters toward a communal campfire to capture some of the heat inside the shelter. The floor of the shelter consisted of more thick layers of pine boughs, upon which the soldier lay wrapped in a bearskin blanket.

The secret to trail life in the American wilderness was simplicity. Simplicity was reflected in the fact that only the most essential gear was carried:

TERRAIN AND LIVING CONDITIONS

The wilderness of the United States is an unforgiving terrain for those living rough. The soldiers of the American Revolutionary War, on both sides, had to contend with extreme environments in the depths of winter and the heights of summer.

The experience of soldiering during the Revolutionary War was rarely harder than that suffered by the Continental Army in the first few years of the war. Meanly resourced, underfed, poorly dressed, and badly trained, the American soldier found himself attempting to survive in the frozen valleys and endless woodlands of Eastern America.

SURVIVAL AND ADAPTATION

During the winter of 1777–78, a large part of the Continental Army took winter quarters at Valley Forge,

▼ The famous Molly Pitcher, reputed to have helped rebel troops at the Battle of Monmouth, New Jersey, 1778. Note the ragged state of the clothing.

"We are in **the most damnable country**, this land is fit only for **wolves and its native savages**."

A BRITISH OFFICER OF THE 55TH FOOT, LAKE GEORGE, 1758

EYEWITNESS ACCOUNT

"Soon I came in sight of the camp. My imagination had pictured an army with uniforms, the glitter of arms, standards, etc., in short, military pomp of all sorts; Instead of the imposing spectacle I expected, I saw, grouped together or standing alone, a few militiamen, poorly clad, and for the most part without shoes —many of them badly armed, but all well supplied with provisions, and I noticed that tea and sugar formed part of their rations."
—Chevalier de Pontgibaud, Valley Forge, 1777

northeast of Philadelphia. Such was the terrible supply situation that some 3,000 men were unable to serve because they had no footwear and little clothing. They were filthy—soap supplies had dried up—and suffering from exposure. Every man was half starving from lack of meat and vegetables, and a severe shortage of muskets and gunpowder meant that the troops were seriously considering using bows and arrows.

ON CAMPAIGN

Fortunately for the Continental Army, conditions improved as the war progressed, although they never achieved anything approaching luxury. In winter, in areas where timber was plentiful, the soldiers constructed wooden huts, which held 12 men or one to four officers, depending on their seniority. The camps might achieve a semipermanent basis into the summer months, enabling the troops to establish something approaching a social life, including theatrical performances. Music from banjos, penny whistles, and fiddles flowed around the trees and huts, bringing what must have been some light relief on dark nights or around a summer campfire.

▲ George Washington meets with the Marquis de Lafayette at Valley Forge, where the Continental Army endured terrible suffering in the winter of 1777–78.

▼ Campfires were essential for cooking and warmth, yet the long-term breathing of wood smoke led to numerous chest infections and even some types of cancer.

When on the move, accommodation switched to tents, or in the high summer months soldiers sometimes just slept outside on a blanket laid on the ground, relying on the smoke from a smoldering fire to keep away woodland biting insects. When troops were moving through complicated wooded or mountainous terrain, the total distance traveled might be little more than 5 miles/8 km a day, but typically an army would expect to travel more than double this distance. In one epic speed march, American troops at Brandywine marched 5 miles/8 km in just 45 minutes. When they stopped, men rotated through the boredom of camp guard duty every three nights.

Health was a critical issue for soldiers in both barracks and on campaign. Disease inflicted huge casualties on the men, but this situation improved significantly in 1777, when the Continental Army soldiers began to receive vaccinations against smallpox, one of the biggest killers of soldiers during the 18th century.

UNIFORMS AND KIT

The soldiers of this conflict displayed an inconsistent variety of kit and uniform. The battlefield pressure-tested such items to destruction, and resulted in many soldiers making personal adaptations to the things they wore or carried.

The uniform of the regular British soldier was largely predictable, especially compared to the more creative and variable appearance of the Continental Army.

BRITISH FORMALITY

Although the British made some concessions to the camouflage and comfort of uniforms during the 18th century, mainly for their light infantry units, the fact remained that the standard British uniform of the American Revolutionary War was stiff and uncompromising. Summarizing broadly, it featured a heavy red wool coat, vest, breeches, gaiters, and leather shoes. Everything about the outfit was tight and uncomfortable, and it tended to exacerbate both cold and heat in equal measures.

▲ Reenactors depict the British retreat from Concord. The tricorne hats were common items among both British and rebels.

◄ About six or seven men might share a cast-iron cooking pot, with individuals bringing kettles and cooking utensils.

▼ Light was supplied by oil lamps (1) or storm lanterns (2).

In terms of kit, the soldier had a cartridge box on his right hip (hanging from a shoulder strap), a bayonet scabbard on a belt, and a haversack containing all practical items, including shoe cleaning kit, musketry equipment, cooking pots and eating utensils, some tent equipment (one tent's worth of equipment was distributed between five men) plus personal effects. The regimented appearance hid much muscle pain, chafing, and overheating.

CONTINENTAL ARMY DRESS

Clothing and equipment in the Continental Army was more inconsistent, as the emerging nation struggled to provide its men with a uniform. For the first two years, men dressed simply in what was available, with some regiments approaching standardized clothing while others displayed a haphazard mix of hunting attire and work clothes. Hunting shirts actually remained popular items throughout the war, being highly practical in the field and also protecting any official uniform items from wear and tear.

In September 1777, Congress issued its first uniform allowance regulations: 1 coat, 1 vest, 1 pair of buckskin and 2 pairs of linen breeches; 1 hat/leather cap; 2 shirts; 1 hunting shirt; 2 pairs of overalls; 2 pairs of shoes; 1 blanket. The coat color was brown, but from 1778 blue coats were also worn, which were imported from France.

Although the Continental Army looked rough and ready, many of its uniform items were far kinder to the wearers than the British equivalents. The uniform was also supplemented by anything the soldier could find or capture. Equipment was held in a backpack (for clothing, blanket, and personal belongings) with three days' rations in a small haversack.

▼ An idealized picture of military costumes of the Revolution. George Washington (center) is surrounded by four soldiers in European uniforms.

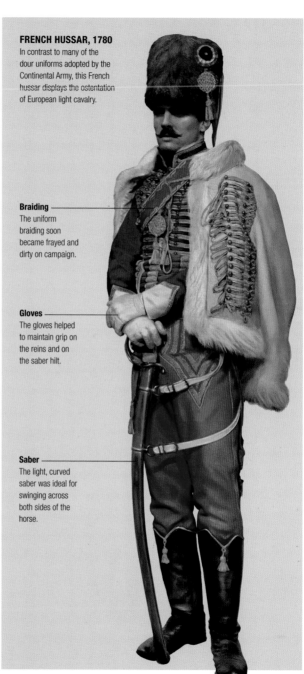

FRENCH HUSSAR, 1780
In contrast to many of the dour uniforms adopted by the Continental Army, this French hussar displays the ostentation of European light cavalry.

Braiding
The uniform braiding soon became frayed and dirty on campaign.

Gloves
The gloves helped to maintain grip on the reins and on the saber hilt.

Saber
The light, curved saber was ideal for swinging across both sides of the horse.

FACETS OF WAR: COMMUNICATIONS

Communications are what turn a collection of individual soldiers into a cohesive and coordinated unit. But the ability to communicate rapidly across distance has evolved slowly, dependent on seminal steps in technology.

Achieving effective battlefield communication has been a persistent challenge at the heart of military operations. Active combat zones are noisy and confusing places, and commanders have long sought the means to cut through the din and fog of battle and deliver coherent instructions to their units.

VISUAL AND AUDIBLE MEANS

From ancient times to the 19th century, the principal tools for battlefield communications were visual and audible. Regarding the latter, the voice was the most immediate, although it required considerable volume—hence the parade-ground shrieking of drill sergeants. But the voice was easily lost among other sounds, therefore musical instruments—especially drums, brass

instruments, and whistles/pipes—were used to deliver coded messages at a more substantial volume.

In visual terms, flags, banners, and standards provided a basic means of unit orientation (one reason why an enemy would be keen to capture

▲ Continental Army infantry make a coordinated night attack in 1779, relying on visual communications from an officer.

▼ In World War I, carrier pigeons were an essential means of long-range communication with HQs.

Ready   A or 1   B or 2   C or 3   D or 4   E or 5

F or 6   G or 7   H or 8   I or 9   J   K or 0   L

M   N   O   P   Q   R   S

T   U   V   W   X   Y   Z

◀ Military semaphore. Semaphore provides a means for transmitting precise worded instructions. Its disadvantages are that the enemy can also read the message and that the signaler is highly visible—a tempting target for snipers.

telephone, which would be an essential communication tool throughout World War I. Yet it was the practical refinements of wireless communications —radio—in the 1920s that gave commanders the greatest means for real-time and mobile communications. From the seed of radio, we now have a networked battlefield, although the fog of battle persists.

▲ German radio operators on the Eastern Front during World War II. Field radios were also useful for intercepting enemy radio traffic.

▼ U.S. Marines communicate with their patrol base during a security patrol near the Nahr-e Saraj canal in Helmand, Afghanistan.

the opponent's standards), but other methods included hand signals, fires, and heliograph signaling devices (the latter refined in the 19th century). Flag semaphore was invented in 1794, and was subsequently used heavily by the world's navies and also adopted by army formations.

ELECTRONIC REVOLUTION

The true revolutions in military communications began in the 19th century. The invention of electrical telegraphy in the first half of the century, allied to Morse code, transformed the dissemination of operational commands, even across continents. By the 1880s, the invention of the telephone had also gravitated into military use in the form of the field

A PEOPLE'S WAR

Being civil war as much as colonial conflict, the American Revolutionary War affected every sector of society. Each person, whether or not he or she knew it, had a part to play in the development and outcome of the war and the subsequent founding of a nation.

The Revolutionary War was very much a people's war. The composition of rebel militias and the Continental Army blurred the lines between soldiers and civilians, especially as many soldiers still had civilian duties to perform in nearby farms or businesses. For women and children, and those who stayed out of uniform, the effects on their lives ran from the minor to the catastrophic.

DISRUPTION

As with all conflicts, the Revolutionary War imposed varying levels of disruption. For a start, it inevitably

▼ Samuel Adams, one of the architects of the Revolutionary War, leads a group forcing the resignation of a British official trying to implement the Stamp Act.

▲ An emotive painting of American citizens defending their homes and families against a predatory British Army raid; the man in the center is loading his flintlock.

brought civilians into contact with war-weary soldiers, both friend and enemy, with all the unpredictable social interactions that entailed. Claiming the emergencies of war, passing armies would frequently confiscate food and goods from civilians already rendered desperate by the war's disruptions to trade (such as the closure of local markets) and the British naval blockade. There were also cases of theft by soldiers who were billeted in domestic properties. In some cases soldiers were hanged for stealing, but in most instances the civilian population had little recourse to justice, despite promises to the contrary.

Yet close civilian contact with enemy soldiers also afforded many opportunities for espionage in this

CULPER SPY RING

The Culper Spy Ring was a famous rebel spy network established in New York in 1778. It was led by cavalry officer Benjamin Tallmadge, whom Washington appointed the head of the Continental Army's secret service. It was named after the alias (Samuel Culper) of senior spy Abraham Woodhull, one of Tallmadge's closest associates and friends.

► The Continental Army relied heavily on women assisting field surgeons, allocating one nurse to every ten patients.

country of divided loyalties. On occasion, female spies would hang out their washing in an agreed configuration, the pattern of clothes giving coded information about the numbers or disposition of the troops stationed in their village or town.

▼ Where it all began. The Boston Tea Party in 1773 was a civilian protest against taxation, which swelled into a full-blown revolution.

THE ROLE OF WOMEN

Women served both rebel and British armies directly in the conflict. Some 20 percent of British soldiers brought family members, and in the Continental Army Washington reluctantly allowed the presence of camp followers, as it prevented some soldiers deserting or asking for furloughs to look after destitute wives and children. Women were generally put to work nursing, cleaning, doing laundry, and mending clothes, services for which they could charge the soldiers. The Continental Army issued regulations warning female laundry workers not to overcharge serving personnel, the penalty for doing so being expulsion from the military camp. Women would also do much of the catering, although in many cases they cooked for civilian support personnel rather than the soldiers, who did their own cooking.

LEADERS AND COMMANDERS

This was a conflict in which some men had greatness decidedly and rather unexpectedly thrust upon them. For others the war suddenly, and sometimes violently, stripped them of their authority and reputation, the price of defeat in battle.

Although senior leaders might seem somewhat remote from the daily realities of soldiering, it is worth reminding ourselves of the lives and characters of the men at the summit of the command chain. The American Revolutionary War is fascinating in this regard, as the spectrum of aptitudes and backgrounds among the leaders on both sides was colorful.

SOURCING OFFICERS

There were some key overarching differences between the leaders of the British and Continental forces. For the British, its officers were the

▼ The Marquis de Lafayette, a French officer, came to America in 1777 and took up service with the Continental Army.

▲ George Washington, left, with other officers. As well as being a capable commander, Washington also had a deserved reputation for political cunning.

◄ Washington's mess kit. The mess kit of regular soldiers would be very different, consisting of little more than a kettle, pan, and spoon.

products of the professional officer class, although the system of purchasing commissions meant that they could still be as inept as the officers of any other army. The Continental Army, by contrast, was created before a system of officer recruitment and training could be formalized and refined. Hence the rebel officers tended to be of uncertain quality, some from military backgrounds but others straight from civilian life. Those who had never soldiered before had to be quick learners.

DANIEL MORGAN

Colonel Daniel Morgan (1736–1802) was a superb rebel leader and tactician, known for his fast-marching units and irregular style of warfare. In his prewar military service, he had received 499 lashes for punching a British officer.

> ## "As to war, I am and always was **a great enemy**, at the same time **a warrior** the greater part of my life."
>
> BRIGADIER-GENERAL DANIEL MORGAN, 1758

COMMANDING NAMES

The great leaders of the rebel forces were a mixed bunch of personalities. At the top of the tree, George Washington was an aristocrat from Virginia who had led a regiment (maximum 2,000 men) in the French and Indian Wars, but in 1775 he found himself in charge of a land army of 15,000 men, after a period of 20 years out of uniform.

Like Washington, many rebel commanders had formerly been in the service of the British, such as General Horatio Gates. Conversely, General Benedict Arnold began service with the rebels, but then defected to the British. Some rebel commanders brought little in the way of military experience, but plenty in terms of character. General Anthony Wayne, for example, prior to the war was a land surveyor and tannery owner from Pennsylvania's upper classes. Yet in 1776 he was commissioned as a colonel in the Continental Army, earning the nickname "Mad Anthony" for his fighting spirit when storming the British fort at Stony Point, New York on July 16, 1779.

Some commanders achieved lasting fame for ingenuity as much as command talent. On the British side, Major Patrick Ferguson invented the first British breech-loading service rifle. The .615-in Ferguson was accurate and fired at twice the rate of a regular musket, but the cost of its manufacture limited its general distribution.

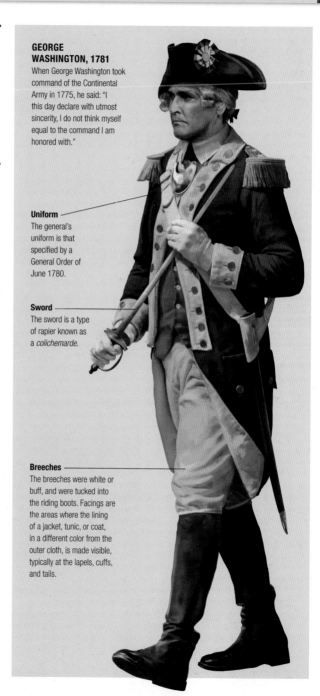

GEORGE WASHINGTON, 1781

When George Washington took command of the Continental Army in 1775, he said: "I this day declare with utmost sincerity, I do not think myself equal to the command I am honored with."

Uniform
The general's uniform is that specified by a General Order of June 1780.

Sword
The sword is a type of rapier known as a *colichemarde*.

Breeches
The breeches were white or buff, and were tucked into the riding boots. Facings are the areas where the lining of a jacket, tunic, or coat, in a different color from the outer cloth, is made visible, typically at the lapels, cuffs, and tails.

> "I thought **one could wish for** nothing better **than to fight** against **all possible odds.**"
>
> JEAN-BAPTISTE BARRÈS, FRENCH SOLDIER

THE NAPOLEONIC WARS

1789–1815

In 1789, France was convulsed, and transformed, by revolution. But this was not just an internal upheaval. The revolution triggered a series of major wars that rumbled across Europe and other parts of the world for more than two decades. From 1803, the man at the center of the conflict was the infamous Napoleon Bonaparte.

◄ French cavalry make a charge during the Battle of La Fère-Champenoise, March 25, 1814. At this stage in history, cavalry could be a battle-deciding force, delivering shock attacks at great speed against exposed enemy lines.

THE RISE OF THE MASS ARMIES

The armies of the Napoleonic Wars were forged in tradition and tempered by modernity. Tradition was on vivid display in uniforms and regimental pride, while modern tactical approaches were demanded by the scale and intensity of the warfare.

The label "Napoleonic Wars" is pegged to the activities of arguably the greatest military commander in history—Napoleon Bonaparte (1769–1821). From a relatively humble artillery officer in the French Army, Napoleon rose to prominence as a loyal and highly competent leader during the internal and international wars following the French Revolution of 1789. He grabbed the headlines with his deft command in battles and campaigns such as Toulon (1793), Arcola (1796), and Egypt (1798), but he was also politically adept. In 1799 he became France's First Consul and within five years had crowned himself emperor.

Napoleon set Europe ablaze at the head of one of the largest and most impressive armies the continent had even seen. With a gift for rapid, aggressive tactical maneuvers, Napoleon wielded his forces to win great victories

▶ French light cavalry engage Russian cossacks during the campaign of 1812, firing their carbines from the saddle.

. . . .

"On these occasions, too, the faces of the bravest often change color."

BRITISH OFFICER, ON THE EVE OF BATTLE

. . . .

▼ Prussian hussars spend moments in discussion during a night picket. Hussars were regarded as the most dashing of cavalry troops.

that still stand as defining moments in military history. Yet he suffered some catastrophic defeats too, such as Borodino in Russia, 1812, and at Waterloo, 1815, the battle that finally crushed Napoleon's dreams of empire and consigned him to exile on the Atlantic island of St. Helena.

MASS ARMIES

The Napoleonic Wars drew in armies from across Europe. The continent's forces had to expand to scales of manpower and firepower little seen in their history. For the invasion of Russia in 1812, Napoleon's troops (including soldiers from Poland, Austria, the Netherlands, Italy, Switzerland, and Denmark) numbered 614,000 men, with a supply train of 25,000 horse-drawn vehicles. The British Army increased to a strength of about 300,000 men in 1813, from 50,000

in 1789. Prussia developed a similar-sized force by 1806. This massive surge in manpower, however, brought a knotty range of logistical, training, and discipline issues. While each army had its core of veteran regular soldiers, many newcomers joined the armed forces with little more incentive than to escape poverty or prison. The formidable British commander Arthur Wellesley, 1st Duke of Wellington, once famously remarked of the common British men-at-arms: "We have in service the scum of the earth as common soldiers."

COURAGE IN BATTLE

As many generals discovered, the most unpromising human material could eventually be crafted into astonishing soldiers. Wellington's soldiers might have been labeled "scum" by their own general, but when called upon they provided numerous volunteers for the "forlorn hope," the men who would be the first to storm a breach in a fortification, with the near certainty of death. The Prussian Army also rose from crushing defeats to victories at Leipzig (1813) and Waterloo (1815).

▲ Napoleon's encampment at Abersberg Castle, as seen in 1809. Napoleon had a gift for decisive strategic and tactical thinking, and was adored by many of his troops.

▼ On the evening of the Battle of Waterloo, by Ernest Crofts, shows something of the chaos of the Napoleonic battlefield. Soldiers would often be crushed or trampled by panicked, riderless horses.

The armies of the Napoleonic era remained hierarchical. But, as Napoleon himself indicated, a new meritocracy was creeping in, particularly among the officer class. Furthermore, technical arms such as engineers and the artillery were becoming increasingly important. It took another century for these changes to develop, but the Napoleonic Wars indicated that character, not position, could be decisive.

THE FRENCH ARMY

From its humble conscripts to the officers of noble birth, the French Army coalesced into an effective fighting force under Napoleon that swept almost all its opponents aside.

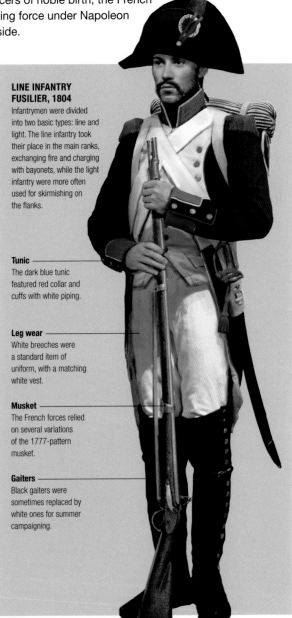

The French Revolution, and the conflicts it spawned, produced a near insatiable requirement for military manpower in France. To meet this requirement, mass conscription was introduced in August 1793. All able-bodied men between ages 18 and 25 were eligible for call-up. Thousands of men chose to avoid the draft through desertion or other means, such as paying another person to act as a substitute. Nonetheless, the draft resulted in a surge of men into the ranks, 1.5 million by the end of the year.

INFANTRY

The French Army, like other European armies of the time, was split into three broad classifications of combat troops: infantry (which formed the bulk), artillery, and cavalry. Organized (from 1803) into regiments, battalions, and companies, the infantry was a somewhat ragged force. Prior to Napoleon's command, revolutionary France had problems feeding and clothing so many men, and pay could be haphazard. Conditions improved steadily in the 1800s, with better standardization of uniforms and

"The **French charged** with shouldered arms, as was their custom... **the English remained motionless.**"

FRENCH SOLDIER, 1814

LINE INFANTRY FUSILIER, 1804
Infantrymen were divided into two basic types: line and light. The line infantry took their place in the main ranks, exchanging fire and charging with bayonets, while the light infantry were more often used for skirmishing on the flanks.

Tunic
The dark blue tunic featured red collar and cuffs with white piping.

Leg wear
White breeches were a standard item of uniform, with a matching white vest.

Musket
The French forces relied on several variations of the 1777-pattern musket.

Gaiters
Black gaiters were sometimes replaced by white ones for summer campaigning.

Bearskin
The bearskin was a heavy and impractical hat, particularly when wet and dirty.

FRENCH SAPPER, 1807
The blue tunic of this sapper, as opposed to the gray uniforms worn by many members of the auxiliary engineer corps, marks him out as a member of a line regiment.

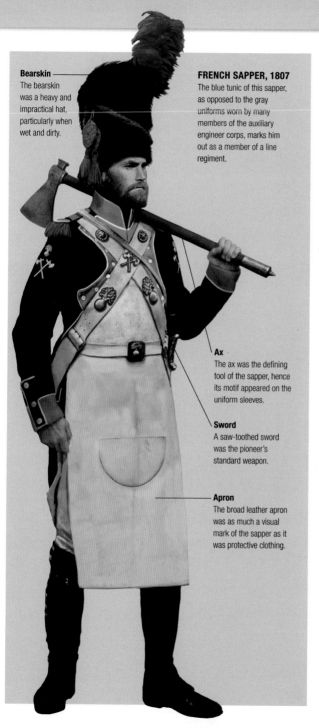

Ax
The ax was the defining tool of the sapper, hence its motif appeared on the uniform sleeves.

Sword
A saw-toothed sword was the pioneer's standard weapon.

Apron
The broad leather apron was as much a visual mark of the sapper as it was protective clothing.

▲ Cavalry charges were powerful assaults if coordinated well, although casualties to men and mounts were high from artillery and musket fire.

equipment. Yet the French infantry remained hard-pressed. In later years thousands of teenagers, nicknamed "Marie-Louises," were pressed into service to fill the gaps left by casualties.

CAVALRY AND ARTILLERY

The cavalry were the most dashing and self-consciously elite of Napoleon's forces, divided into "light" and "heavy" arms. The light cavalry (hussars, chasseurs, and lancers) were used for reconnaissance, raiding, and infantry support, while the heavy cavalry were defined by the cuirassiers, men who wore hefty metal breastplates—"cuirasses"—and wielded sabers; their specialty was delivering thunderous charges to break enemy ranks.

The artillery, however, was one of the most influential branches of the French Army. Reforms in the 1760s had dramatically increased the number of eight- and twelve-pounder field guns in the frontline forces. Napoleon wielded his horse-drawn field artillerymen with great dexterity, inflicting terrible casualties on opposing troops.

ANTI-FRENCH ALLIES

Opposing the imperial ambition of the French was a broad spectrum of allied forces, offering varying degrees of manpower, professionalism, and leadership. It was the combined strength of this coalition that ultimately led to Napoleon's defeat in 1815.

The allegiances of the Napoleonic Wars were shifting entities. For example, at certain stages of the conflict, Austria, Russia, and Prussia—three of Europe's greatest armies—fought for the French as client states, but also for the anti-French alliance. The shift to the latter became most pronounced in the last two years of the conflict, once Napoleon had been critically weakened by defeat in Russia in 1812. The qualities of each army, and the soldiers within, were therefore vulnerable to politics and strategic decisions. The Austrian Army, for instance, suffered from problems in reforming its military structures, affecting morale and living conditions for the average soldier that didn't improve until around 1807. Prussia had a strong tradition of martial spirit and discipline, but tactically it

▲ A British Redcoat reenactor lets off a shot with his Brown Bess musket. His headgear is the classic plumed shako.

▼ Typical items in a British soldier's kit: 1 checkers set; 2 metal polish; 3 leather polish; 4 compass; 5 button stick; 6 washing and shaving kit; 7 pocket knife; 8 sewing kit; 9 flint, steel, and tinder.

was somewhat outdated during the first decade of the conflict, and had been virtually destroyed in battle by 1806. From this low point, however, Prussia managed to rebuild its manpower and tactical edge, and ultimately played a critical part in Napoleon's final defeat at Waterloo.

BRITAIN

The most constant enemy of France throughout this period was Britain. At its heart were the infantry "Redcoats," so called after the red coats they wore, unhelpfully crossed with white straps that provided a perfect target for enemy shooters. Although the British soldier was often recruited from some of the most unsoldierly material across the British Isles, through hard training and severe discipline he tended to become a stalwart trooper, fiercely loyal to his regiment and battalion. British soldiers were known for their stoical resilience under fire, and their frenzied violence in hand-to-hand fighting. The officers of the British forces tended to be of high birth and financial means—the latter was essential to make progress through the officer ranks, as commissions were largely dependent on purchasing power. Yet the Napoleonic Wars did provide opportunity for many humbler men to distinguish themselves through action.

RUSSIA

Russian soldiers were, from 1793, recruited into the ranks for 25 years. In contrast to the British, they took their place in a vast, sprawling force that was generally under-resourced, poorly armed, and badly led. Common soldiers tended to be poor and illiterate serfs, and junior officers often had little military knowledge. Senior officers were pure aristocracy, often disconnected from the daily lives of the soldiers. Like many armies, however, reforms from around 1806 slightly improved the lot of the Russian soldier, with better logistics and improved muskets.

▼ Officers of the King's German Legion (KGL) relax on campaign. The KGL was an expatriate German force that served under British command.

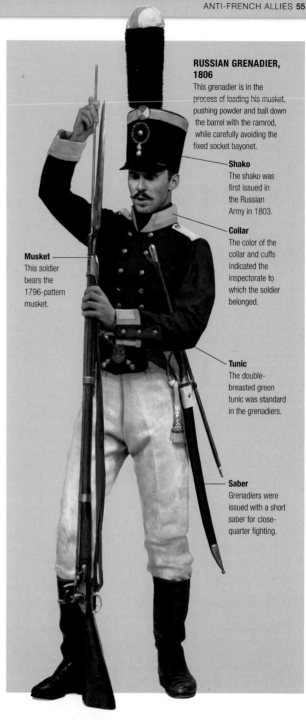

RUSSIAN GRENADIER, 1806
This grenadier is in the process of loading his musket, pushing powder and ball down the barrel with the ramrod, while carefully avoiding the fixed socket bayonet.

Shako
The shako was first issued in the Russian Army in 1803.

Collar
The color of the collar and cuffs indicated the inspectorate to which the soldier belonged.

Musket
This soldier bears the 1796-pattern musket.

Tunic
The double-breasted green tunic was standard in the grenadiers.

Saber
Grenadiers were issued with a short saber for close-quarter fighting.

HANDHELD FIREPOWER

Not long after fighting commenced, the battlefield would be shrouded in a dense fog of gun smoke, rippling with the flashes of pan and muzzle. Individual accuracy with a gun mattered less than the ability to reload and fire in quick volleys.

In today's era of super-accurate rifles, it is hard to appreciate the random nature of Napoleonic-era muskets. Although some infantrymen, typically elite light-infantry types, did receive marksmanship training, most other soldiers had little or no such instruction. This was not necessarily an oversight, but realism. Muskets in themselves were highly inaccurate weapons. Even against broad-area targets, a musket's effective range was likely 100 yards/ 91 m or less. In some European tests, it was found that 50 percent of shots missed a large canvas screen when fired at 150 yards/164 m, and even at 75 yards/68.5 m up to 30 percent were still wide of the mark.

VOLLEY FIRE

It was for this reason that volley fire—firing repeated coordinated shots from serried ranks—was utilized. The theory

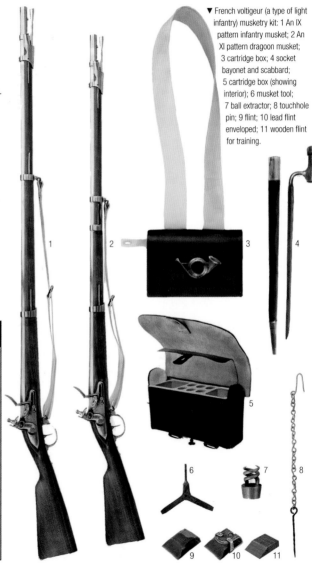

▼ French voltigeur (a type of light infantry) musketry kit: 1 An IX pattern infantry musket; 2 An XI pattern dragoon musket; 3 cartridge box; 4 socket bayonet and scabbard; 5 cartridge box (showing interior); 6 musket tool; 7 ball extractor; 8 touchhole pin; 9 flint; 10 lead flint enveloped; 11 wooden flint for training.

EYEWITNESS ACCOUNT

"An infantry fire fight was a brutal, jostling affair. When your priming sparked, you got a small shower of half-burnt powder grains and flint particles in your face. Your musket kicked savagely; with three ranks of men firing, the center rank would be jostled, with many shots going wild... It was dry, harried work; muskets slamming all around you, smoke in your eyes. Biting cartridges dried out your mouth..."
—A French soldier, quoted in *Tactics and Experience in the Age of Napoleon*, by Dr. Rory Muir.

was that although individual accuracy was poor, group firing could still achieve powerful effects on the closely packed enemy ranks.

TOOLS OF WAR

The early 19th-century musket was a flintlock design with a smooth (not

◀ A foot chasseur of the French Imperial Guard tears open a cartridge with his teeth. Ingestion of gunpowder could cause intense feelings of nausea during battle.

....

"**Inexperienced officers** have repeatedly given orders to **commence a fire**, without either **judgment** or consideration..."

BRITISH VETERAN OF THE PENINSULAR WAR

....

▲ After the first volley, it became increasingly hard for officers to keep the fire coordinated. Repeated firing might make the soldiers "gun-shy" as their shoulders became bruised.

rifled) bore—hence the gun's general inaccuracy. The cavalry would use shortened muskets, known as carbines, plus pistols.

Typical muskets, such as the French Charleville or the British "Brown Bess," measured about 60 inches/150 cm and weighed some 10 pounds/4.5 kg. Handling one of these weapons consistently in a volley was no easy matter. As the barrel became fouled with gunpowder deposits it became increasingly hard to reload the musket ball, slowing the rate of fire. There was also the sheer unreliability of the weapons. Even in perfect weather with good flints, up to 15 percent of shots could be anxious misfires; double that figure in wet weather. So what began as a coordinated volley could descend into ragged firing at will. Closing with bayonets was often advisable, as sharpened steel was at least reliable.

NAPOLEONIC GUNNERS

Operating Napoleonic artillery pieces was a hard business—physically demanding, brutally noisy, and often lethally dangerous. It also required men of technical expertise, who could handle the complex engines of war under battlefield pressures.

Artillery had been in use for several centuries by the time of the Napoleonic Wars, but these conflicts served to heighten its importance. The guns themselves were broadly divided into two categories: heavy guns suited to static defense, or lighter field guns used to provide semimobile firepower. The field guns were subdivided according to horse or foot artillery.

HORSE AND FOOT ARTILLERY

Horse artillery crews generally regarded themselves as the most dashing members of the artillery arm, with uniforms that imitated those of the lofty hussars. Horse artillery guns were pulled into position by horses, and their crews were also mounted. This meant that artillery could be deployed quickly to points of crisis and opportunity, and a good crew was able to have the gun unlimbered and into action in less than a minute.

Foot artillery had a rather more stoic and less glamorous role. Although the guns and associated supplies would still be pulled by horses, the crews themselves moved on foot. The foot artillery would generally be in more fixed defensive or supporting positions on the battlefield.

> "Soldiers like the **noise of Artillery**; it gives them **confidence** when employed in **their support**."
>
> BRITISH OFFICER LIEUTENANT-COLONEL DICKSON, c.1816

◄ The Battle of Waterloo, 1815, and as Wellington issues orders in the background, a foot artillery unit struggles to control its horses while deploying a nine-pounder field gun.

ARTILLERY EFFECTS

Guns fired either roundshot (solid metal balls), canister (a sheet metal box filled with musket balls or heavier "grape" shot), or exploding shrapnel shells. All these types of ammunition had a horrific effect on targets. Tests in 1812 found that a twelve-pounder roundshot was capable of penetrating more than a dozen humans at a range of 600–700 yards/550–640 m. Roundshot was often fired so that it skipped along the ground, scything through the ranks of the enemy.

▲ A gunner belonging to the horse artillery of the French Garde Imperiale feeds a roundshot into a short-barreled field artillery piece.

THE GUNNER'S EXPERIENCE

An artilleryman's life could be as precarious and grinding as that of the infantryman. Typically, engagement ranges would be 250–600 yards/ 230–550 m, and the batteries would attract counterfire from enemy artillery and would also be a key focus for enemy cavalry assaults. The constant process of loading and firing the guns was physically exhausting, and crews would be bathed in sweat, stinking of gunpowder, and deafened by the constant percussions. Yet even in the midst of battle, they had to stay aware. Sparks from the guns could cause grass fires that might detonate gunpowder; rates of fire had to be adjusted for the barrels as they heated up (one or two rounds a minute was a typical rate of fire). Generally speaking, during a major battle an individual gun might fire between 100 and 150 rounds.

The technical skills of artillery were regarded as somewhat demeaning by the highest military ranks, hence it was not the service of choice for such men looking to take a commission. Yet the influence and importance of artillery personnel would grow inexorably.

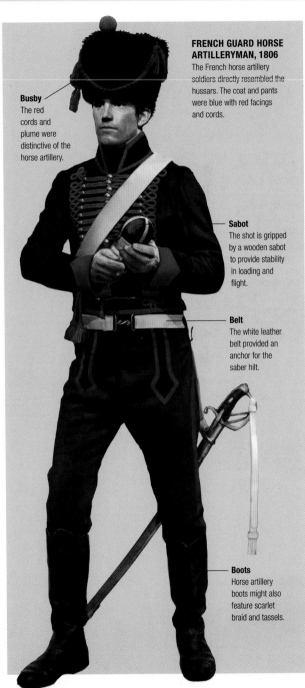

FRENCH GUARD HORSE ARTILLERYMAN, 1806
The French horse artillery soldiers directly resembled the hussars. The coat and pants were blue with red facings and cords.

Busby
The red cords and plume were distinctive of the horse artillery.

Sabot
The shot is gripped by a wooden sabot to provide stability in loading and flight.

Belt
The white leather belt provided an anchor for the saber hilt.

Boots
Horse artillery boots might also feature scarlet braid and tassels.

CAMP LIFE

Armies of the Napoleonic era campaigned far from their homelands, in places of unfamiliar language, food, and terrain. Camps were the only place that the soldiers could call their own, even if such settlements were decidedly temporary.

Camp life during a Napoleonic-era campaign was, needless to say, rarely comfortable. The degree of comfort, however, depended somewhat upon the logistical approach of a particular army and the operational conditions in which it found itself.

ORGANIZED LOGISTICS

The Austrians, a relatively well-equipped military force, had a regimented approach to the way they put a camp together and kept themselves supplied. Every individual had a fur-covered leather backpack

▼ French reenactors present an authentic image of camp cooking. Rice and bread were typically the only foods the French carried as standard; the rest was foraged.

▲ A reconstruction of a Prussian army camp setting. The footlocker appears to contain personal items for a female camp follower.

known as a "tornister." This contained all the soldier's personal items, including hairband and comb, cleaning kit, knife and fork, and shoe polish. Each regiment of troops had 534 tents, one for every five men, and these were carried on wagons and packhorses. The supply train also carried a prescribed number of straw bundles and wooden planking, both used to line the floors of the tents. A problem was that on a long campaign the tents often became rain-soaked and rotted. Nevertheless, the Austrians were able to erect a decent camp at the end of a march.

THE FRENCH APPROACH

French armies, at least when campaigning in Western Europe, took a somewhat different approach to

camp life. Preferring the advantages of rapid movement over heavy and slow supply trains, the French would often go on campaign without tents. When they needed to set up an overnight base, they would construct shelters out of any local materials available, or commandeer accommodation nearby. Food depended on successful foraging from the surrounding area; many a farm would find itself suddenly stripped of crops and livestock by a French regiment passing through.

The "live light" ethos was fine for campaigns in fertile, temperate climates such as Austria and Bavaria, but during the Russian campaign the French Army had to revert to traditional supply trains. These systems steadily broke down as the army journeyed through Poland and Russia, ultimately leaving thousands of men starving and destitute on the retreat from Moscow.

▲ A British soldier's personal kit, as carried in the Caribbean campaigns. The items are: 1 haversack for rations; 2 water bottle; 3 knapsack and bedroll; 4 and 5 cartridge box with cartridges (6); 7 drinking mug; 8 barrel tampion; 9 brass case for a fife; 10 musket lock picker.

....

"It would be impossible to build finer camps than yours, but... you have left some wretched villages."

KING OF PRUSSIA, OBSERVING A FRENCH CAMP

....

The British also, at times, adopted a lighter logistical footprint, particularly in the Peninsular War, where the hot summer nights meant sleeping without cover was often viable. Blankets were often specially designed to be adapted into crude tents, when the situation demanded it.

▼ French soldiers cooking chicken for Napoleon on the day of the Battle of Marengo. In the wider army, civilians often prepared much of the food.

MARCHING AND DEPLOYMENT

Covering great distances by foot was the lot of the soldier in the early 19th century. Sometimes the deployments were made in brisk and spirited fashion, with high morale, while on other occasions they were desperate ordeals in which survival was the only objective.

Moving an army quickly and efficiently was vital. During the Revolutionary and Napoleonic Wars, the armies of Europe were constantly on the move, each trying to use speed of deployment to outmaneuver the enemy.

ON THE MOVE

A marching army, with all its attendant horses, wagons, artillery, and camp followers, was a huge entity to move around. In a major campaign, a force of 30,000 infantry would extend about 5 miles/8 km in good order, but as the formation began to stretch out, it would extend to about 7 miles/11 km. In addition, 6,000 cavalry would require 2.5 miles/4 km of linear space, and a force of 60 artillery pieces the same.

▼ Deep snow and subzero conditions, plus terrain obstacles, could reduce a column's speed of march to about a quarter of what it would be in good conditions.

▲ A typically desperate scene of the French during the Russian campaign of 1812. Here they scratch out a basic overnight camp on the freezing open steppe.

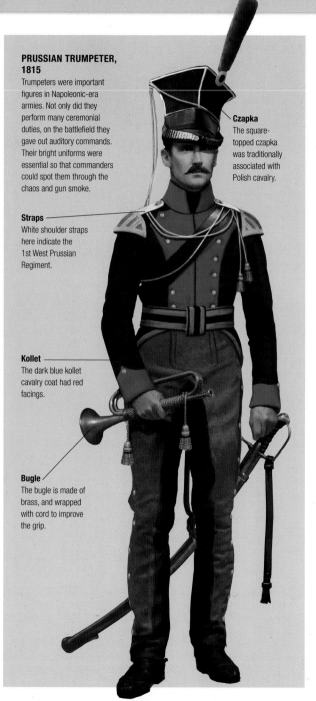

PRUSSIAN TRUMPETER, 1815

Trumpeters were important figures in Napoleonic-era armies. Not only did they perform many ceremonial duties, on the battlefield they gave out auditory commands. Their bright uniforms were essential so that commanders could spot them through the chaos and gun smoke.

Straps

White shoulder straps here indicate the 1st West Prussian Regiment.

Kollet

The dark blue kollet cavalry coat had red facings.

Bugle

The bugle is made of brass, and wrapped with cord to improve the grip.

Czapka

The square-topped czapka was traditionally associated with Polish cavalry.

A primary challenge for commanders was ensuring that such monstrous columns maintained a decent pace. Each soldier would be carrying 55–77 pounds/23–35 kg of kit, and maintaining this load over days of marching produced fatigue, aching joints, and numbness (especially where straps cut off blood supply), as well as problems with worn footwear and clothing, which became soaked with sweat. Naturally, an army could slow significantly over the duration of a long march. Napoleon's solution was to reduce the personal burden of each soldier, which increased their average steps per minute from 70 to 120. This raised the distance they covered from 12 to 19 miles (20 km to 30 km) a day.

ORDEAL

Napoleon's campaign in Russia in 1812 is the crowning example of how a campaign deployment could unravel. Even by the time the French Army had reached Moscow in September, it had already lost a devastating 200,000 men to typhus, dysentery, exhaustion, and combat.

In October, having found no substantial supplies in the largely abandoned city, the French survivors began to retreat, into an exceptionally cruel winter. Tens of thousands of men froze to death on the steppe. Virtually every horse was eaten by the now-starving men—survivors recounted how, the very moment a horse collapsed, the men would swarm on it in a feeding frenzy. Some men attempted to eat their leather equipment; there were even cases of cannibalism.

Of course, the retreat from Moscow was a particularly harrowing event. Yet all major marches were tough, hungry, and tiring experiences. That the soldiers made such journeys in generally impractical uniforms makes them all the more remarkable.

THE PENINSULAR WAR

The Peninsular War, fought between 1808 and 1814, was a unique theater within the overall context of the Napoleonic Wars. It pitted a French expeditionary force against the combined armies of Britain, Portugal, and Spain.

The Peninsular War was the dominant theater for the British for much of the Napoleonic era. In an unfamiliar wilderness and culture, tens of thousands of British troops fought across the plains, rivers, and mountains of the Iberian Peninsula, and in the process secured a reputation for dogged courage under fire.

WILDERNESS AND WAR

The British soldiers deployed to the Peninsular theater were the beneficiaries of first-rate leadership, in the form of Sir Arthur Wellesley, later known as the Duke of Wellington. The logistical challenge he faced within the theater was severe. Unlike the highly fertile lands of Western Europe, large areas of Spain and Portugal were barren and inhospitable, with little food or fodder. Wellington ably negotiated this problem through an effective system of supply from the sea, plus a chain of

▶ The British 15th Hussar Regiment crosses the Zadorra River, prior to the Battle of Vitoria, 1813, a combined British, Spanish, and Portuguese victory.

· ·

"I have **the satisfaction** of reflecting that, having tried them frequently, they have **never failed me.**"

WELLINGTON ON HIS SOLDIERS

· ·

▼ British infantry engage charging French troops with volley fire. If particularly hard-pressed, British troops would form into "square," to make a 360-degree defense.

depots in the interior of the country that could meet demand from multiple locations, so the British soldier in the campaign remained relatively well fed and equipped.

This being said, the Iberian wilderness was still tough on soldiers. The combination of intense heat and sunlight through the summer, then rain and cold during winter, meant that the color quickly bled out of uniforms and leather straps weakened and broke. The shakos worn by the soldiers gave no protection for the eyes from direct sunlight, causing headaches and visual disturbances. Notably, tents were not supplied in quantity until the last year of the war, making the winter months a cruel experience.

UNFORGIVING CAMPAIGNS

The Peninsular War, on many occasions, seemed to bring out the worst in human nature. The usually highly

disciplined British soldiers several times indulged in excessive and systematic acts of violent looting following sieges, such as those at Badajoz (1812) and San Sebastián (1813).

The French were bedeviled constantly by Portuguese and Spanish guerrilla forces, who would descend quickly on an isolated outpost and either kill or capture handfuls of French troops. Those who were unfortunate enough to be captured were frequently tortured and executed, sometimes by vengeful local civilians. At the height of the conflict, the French were losing 25 men every day to guerrilla actions.

To give this context, we must remember that the French also prosecuted a campaign of occupation without mercy. During the siege of Saragossa in 1808–09, for example, French shelling and the spread of typhus killed an estimated 54,000 Spanish citizens, turning Saragossa into a city of corpses. Little quarter was given on any side.

▲ On May 2, 1808, the people of Madrid rose up against French occupation troops. The French took relatively few casualties, but their subsequent executions of prisoners hardened the enmity of the Spanish toward the invaders.

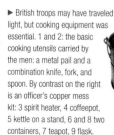

▶ British troops may have traveled light, but cooking equipment was essential. 1 and 2: the basic cooking utensils carried by the men: a metal pail and a combination knife, fork, and spoon. By contrast on the right is an officer's copper mess kit: 3 spirit heater, 4 coffeepot, 5 kettle on a stand, 6 and 8 two containers, 7 teapot, 9 flask.

FACETS OF WAR: LOGISTICS

General Robert H. Barrow, former commandant of the United States Marine Corps, once noted: "Amateurs think about tactics, but professionals think about logistics." It is certainly true that a military commander overlooks logistics at his peril.

Armies have huge matériel demands to maintain their operability in the field. When Napoleon embarked on his ill-fated adventure into Russia in 1812, for example, he strove to establish a supply train that could provide provisions and equipment for 600,000 men and 250,000 horses. A 26-battalion wagon train was provided to deliver an intended 40 days of supplies, the train totaling no fewer than 9,300 individual wagons. Yet despite transporting more than 10,000 tons of supplies, ultimately the wagon train carried less than half what the army actually needed for the campaign, hence some of the terrible problems it later experienced.

LOGISTICAL CALCULATIONS

The soldiers who deliver logistics, and the staff members who plan them, have some of the least glamorous yet most essential roles in the armed forces. They have to engage in intensely complex

▲ France, 1918, a United States supply train moves toward the frontline, still relying on the age-old system of horse and wagon.

▼ A medieval illustration depicts soldiers from the army of Charlemagne (r. 800–814) moving barrels of wine and other provisions in crude open carts.

mathematical calculations, creating formulae with elements that include the size of the army, its predicted consumption of food, ammunition, water, kit, uniform items, medical supplies, fuel, electrical components, and a myriad of other factors. All calculations have to include the duration of the operation, the logistical means available, the cost of buying, delivering, and storing the matériel, and the shelf life of the supplies.

LOGISTICAL MEANS

The simplest means of taking supplies on a campaign is the soldier himself. Back in the 4th century BC, the great commander Philip of Macedon dispensed with much of the traditional baggage train in favor of making his soldiers the principal beasts of burden, to great effect. But soldiers are generally limited to the weight they can carry and still be mobile, so horses, mules, camels, and oxen have been the primary means of heavy logistics for millennia. As a general rule, horses and mules can carry

up to 20 percent of their body weight, meaning the average mule can haul 200 pounds/90 kg of dead weight.

Animal logistics were still important for the first half of the 20th century, but were gradually replaced first by motorized vehicles and rail, and then by airlift, which had massive and tireless hauling capability.

▲ During the Indochina War (1945–54) the Viet Minh were masters of improvised logistics; here rice is transported on bicycles.

▼ Helmand Province, Afghanistan. British Army trucks from the 13 Air Assault Support Regiment, each capable of hauling tons of supplies, about to depart their base.

TIMELINE

700 BC The Assyrians supply the world's first standing army with a baggage train.

4th century BC Alexander the Great utilizes maritime and riverine logistics to support land campaigns.

500–1500 Medieval armies generally have poor logistics, based mostly on foraging.

17th–18th centuries The French take a lead in developing logistics, including using civilian contractors and the magazine system.

19th century The world's expanding road and rail networks assist logistical movement.

1914–45 The two World Wars see the gradual shift from horse-drawn to mechanized logistics.

1945 onward Heavy-lift helicopters transform logistics.

COHESION AND COMRADESHIP

For a regiment or battalion to fight at its best, it needed a strong sense of motivation and an intrinsic belief in its potential to survive. The most powerful cement among soldiers and officers was a shared victory, while defeat and retreat could erode those bonds.

Unified morale had a definite military value for Napoleonic armies. Those regiments and units who possessed such cohesion generally showed the requisite individual daring and courage on the battlefield, even through heavy losses. If such a cohesion disintegrated, the unit was far more likely to yield to an enemy attack, or deliver its own assault with partial commitment.

TRADITION

For all armies, regimental tradition was an extremely strong bond. Men in those regiments that regarded themselves as elite were generally determined to uphold that tradition with their own behavior, on and off the battlefield. Such elites included the French Imperial Guard, the British Royal Horse Artillery, and the Russian Guards regiments. Broadly speaking, the cavalry

▲ The Royal Scots Greys charged as a mass at Waterloo, their shout "Scotland forever!" proclaiming national and unit loyalty.

▼ Civilian support can inspire military cohesion. Here, heroine Johanna Stegen brings ammunition to German troops in 1813.

of almost all armies had a particularly strong sense of their own status. Hussars, for example, tried to live up to their reputation for wild courage, and were equally famous for relentless womanizing off the battlefield.

The cohesive traditions of the regiment were most visibly embodied in the colors or other regimental standards and symbols carried on the battlefield, such as the French imperial eagle. The colors not only provided a visual compass for the unit's maneuvers, they also represented the heart of the unit's pride, a military tradition dating back to Roman times. Men would perform near-suicidal acts of courage to protect them from capture, a shameful occurrence for a regiment. In fact, on some occasions commanders felt the colors would be at too much risk, and kept them to the rear.

VICTORY AND DEFEAT

One of the most profound forces for unit cohesion and comradeship was the experience of victory. The monumental victories of the French at places such

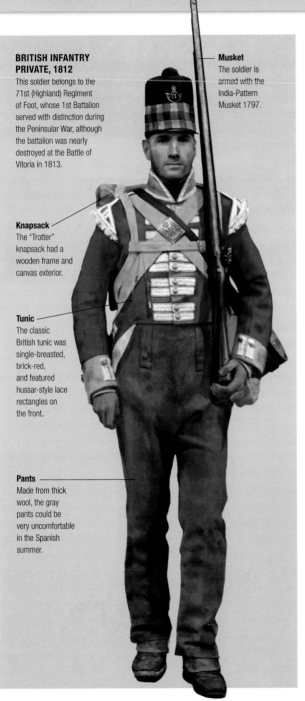

BRITISH INFANTRY PRIVATE, 1812
This soldier belongs to the 71st (Highland) Regiment of Foot, whose 1st Battalion served with distinction during the Peninsular War, although the battalion was nearly destroyed at the Battle of Vitoria in 1813.

Musket
The soldier is armed with the India-Pattern Musket 1797.

Knapsack
The "Trotter" knapsack had a wooden frame and canvas exterior.

Tunic
The classic British tunic was single-breasted, brick-red, and featured hussar-style lace rectangles on the front.

Pants
Made from thick wool, the gray pants could be very uncomfortable in the Spanish summer.

> "A man may **drop behind** in the field but this is a **dreadful risk** to **his reputation**."
>
> SERGEANT ANTON, BRITISH VETERAN, 1813

as Marengo (1800), Ulm (1805), Austerlitz (1805), and Jena (1806), gave the French Army a pervasive sense of its own power, plus a deep-rooted confidence in its commander. Similarly, British victories in the Peninsular War in 1808 demonstrated that the French were not invincible, and delivered an equal surge of self-belief.

Morale and unit cohesion could be fragile qualities, however. Problems with logistics, fatigue, poor leadership, disease, and a lack of rest and recuperation could all weaken unit resolve. It was up to commanders to look after the essential needs of their men to maintain combat effectiveness.

▼ National flags and regimental colors had a galvanizing effect on troops, who generally took pride in national emblems or unit traditions.

DISCIPLINE AND PUNISHMENT

All soldiering requires immense self-discipline. But in the Napoleonic era, military discipline was also imposed externally through a combination of material and physical threats, ranging from docked pay to the death sentence.

Given the size of the Napoleonic-era armies, and their composition from a true cross-section of society, it was inevitable that commanders had to respond to all manner of disciplinary issues. The perennial problems were drunkenness, theft, minor insubordination, poor performance of duties, and unauthorized absences. Although these were widespread, they were treated with hard punishment, the view being that leniency would breed lax discipline throughout a unit.

UNIT PUNISHMENTS

Discipline most obviously trickled down from the unit's officers. In some armies, the level of discipline might border on sadism. In the Russian Army, for example, beatings from officers for the most imperceptible infractions were frequent, giving rise to a common, dark saying about the life of the soldier: "Recruit three, beat to death two, train

> "**Two deserters** from the 7th and 23rd Regiments were **shot before the assembled division. It was a nauseating sight...**"
>
> LIEUTENANT FRIEDRICH VON WACHHOLTZ

▼ Sometimes military units made civilians the focus of retribution and capital punishment. *The Shootings of May 3rd 1808* by Francisco José Goya shows Spanish troops executing local men.

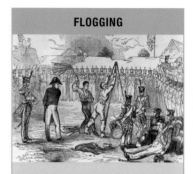

FLOGGING

Flogging was a traditional punishment within many armed services during the 19th century. Typically, the number of lashes was allocated according to the severity of the crime—several hundred might be given for the worst offences, although not all might be delivered in one session. The cat-o'-nine-tails, a whip, or a birch switch were the usual tools of choice.

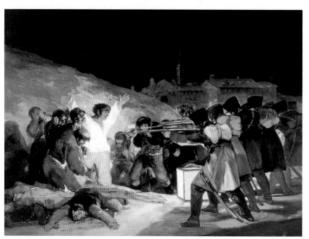

one." But discipline and punishment were also internally imposed by NCOs and the lower ranks. The infractions of one or two individuals could have an impact on the whole company or even battalion, such as canceled leave, so in many cases the unit soldiers would deliver the penalty.

One classic punishment, applied in several armies, was to "run the gauntlet." The victim was stripped to the waist, and forced to walk slowly between two lines of comrades, who would strike and beat him mercilessly with whips and sticks. Another soldier walked in front of him with a fixed bayonet facing rearward, to ensure that

he wasn't tempted to run too quickly. A marginally gentler punishment used in the French Army was to whip the offender 50 times with an old shoe.

CAPITAL CRIMES

For serious crimes, including desertion, mutiny, and murder, soldiers faced capital punishment rather than corporal punishment. This was not an

▲ French cuirassiers charge Scottish Highlanders at Waterloo. The British were famed for the discipline and cohesion they demonstrated in defensive positions.

▼ Discipline in the barracks often expressed itself as resilience in battle. Here, at the Battle of Vimiero (1808), a wounded Highland piper continues to play.

uncommon occurrence—Wellington condemned 112 men to death between 1808 and 1814. The two primary modes of execution in the British Army (and many others) were the firing squad and hanging. Both were grim events. Often, once the offender had been dispatched, the unit would be marched past the dead body, just to hammer home the message about discipline.

EYEWITNESS ACCOUNT

"... the prisoners were drawn to the graveside on a car [cart]. One of them was elderly, the other a boy perhaps nineteen. They kneeled... were blindfolded. All were silent... The provost martial [sic] looks toward the General for the signal. 'Tis given. Twelve men fire. Both culprits fall forward. The boy is dead; the elder rolls in agony. More shots are fired through his head and breast, and the deserters are no more."
—British execution, 1812

THE EXPERIENCE OF WATERLOO

The Battle of Waterloo, fought on June 18, 1815, was the final, epic clash of the Napoleonic Wars. More than 180,000 soldiers fought on that day, in present-day Belgium, with Napoleon's French force pitted against a determined coalition of six other states.

The tactics and events of the Battle of Waterloo have been described in detail by historians over the last two hundred years. However, for the individual soldiers who were actually there that day, the experience would have been far more localized and confusing, as they fought, bled, and died for their own scrap of the battlefield.

LIMITED HORIZONS

Historical accounts of the battle have sometimes given the unfolding events an almost balletic precision, but battlefield descriptions give a very different impression. One key characteristic was limited visibility. The day was largely windless, and the smoke from thousands of muskets and cannon, plus fires at Hougoumont and La Haye Sainte, coalesced in a fairly small area. The men therefore struggled through a choking, hot, and stinking atmosphere, the gloom of the smoke reducing their visibility to a matter of yards, with the only orientation coming largely from muzzle flashes.

The battle space would also have been exceptionally crowded. Just the British forces alone were packed in at a density of 24,000 men per mile. Hence the soldiers fought very closely packed, jostling for space and witnessing the deaths of comrades and enemies at close quarters. To add to the confusion, hundreds of horses thundered about, either cavalry or

▲ Amid scenes of carnage, troops of the Nassau Regiment defend their positions against the French.

▼ French artillery components: 1 ammunition box; 2 water pail; 3–4 shell and sabot; 5 canister; 6–7 grapeshot; 8 rope connecting gun to carriage; 9 priming pins; 10 portfire stick; 11–12 sponge and rammer; 13 worm and ladle tool.

> "I should **not forget**... when **the enemy's artillery** began to play on us...**killing and wounding** great numbers."
>
> CAPTAIN J. H. GRONOW, BRITISH ARMY

horse artillery mounts. One soldier noted that he witnessed opposing cavalry forces meeting one another head-on in a clash. Yet rather than smash into one another—an impact that would have caused heavy casualties on both sides—the ranks parted and passed through one another, as if by mutual consent. In fact, this was common for cavalry encounters, as neither side wanted to incur unnecessary casualties for themselves or their horses.

VIOLENCE IN BATTLE

The sheer violence of that day must have been nerve-shredding. Artillery shot had a devastating impact on the human body, ripping off limbs or opening up ghastly wounds. Indeed it was not uncommon for soldiers to be wounded by the flying bone fragments of someone else struck by shot.

Dead and wounded men littered the ground thickly. For the casualties, their ordeal could be particularly dire. The sheer volume of wounded meant that many of them would not be evacuated to medical help for hours, even days. Casualties were still being discovered up to three days after the battle.

Wellington issued a "Waterloo Medal" to all British soldiers who had fought in this epic struggle, an act that caused some ill-feeling among the many British Peninsular veterans who weren't present for the final battle, but had endured the long campaign.

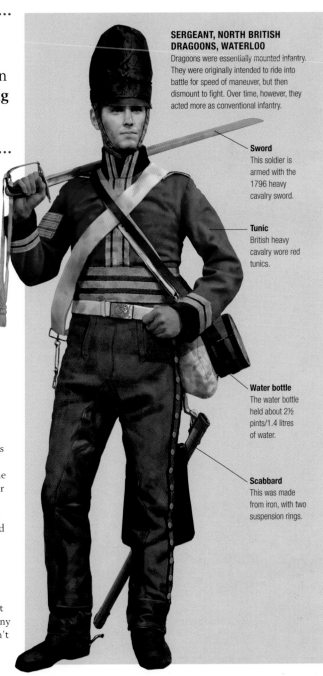

SERGEANT, NORTH BRITISH DRAGOONS, WATERLOO

Dragoons were essentially mounted infantry. They were originally intended to ride into battle for speed of maneuver, but then dismount to fight. Over time, however, they acted more as conventional infantry.

Sword
This soldier is armed with the 1796 heavy cavalry sword.

Tunic
British heavy cavalry wore red tunics.

Water bottle
The water bottle held about 2½ pints/1.4 litres of water.

Scabbard
This was made from iron, with two suspension rings.

THE
AGE OF EMPIRE
AND
STATEHOOD

THE 19TH CENTURY WAS AN ERA OF EMPIRES. ALONGSIDE
THE SPANISH AND THE FRENCH, THE ASCENDANT POWER
WAS GREAT BRITAIN, WHICH RULED OVER ABOUT ONE-
FIFTH OF THE WORLD'S SURFACE. AT THE SAME TIME,
OTHER NATIONS SUCH AS ITALY AND GERMANY WERE
GOING THROUGH THE TRAVAILS OF UNIFICATION, OR IN
THE CASE OF THE UNITED STATES, CIVIL WAR. WITHIN
THESE CONTEXTS, THE NATURE OF SOLDIERING BEGAN ITS
TRUE EVOLUTION TOWARD MODERNITY.

◀ This extraordinary scene from the Crimean War in 1855 shows not only
the noise and chaos of battle but also the fortifications that have been built,
together with the tools and equipment that were used.

"**The art of war** is simple enough.
Find out **where your enemy is**.
Get at him as soon as you can.
Strike him as hard as you can,
and **keep moving on**."

ULYSSES S. GRANT, UNION ARMY GENERAL

THE AMERICAN CIVIL WAR

1861–65

Civil wars bring a unique brand of darkness and brutality. In 1861–65, the soldiers of the northern and southern United States fought for territory and ideology, and combat, disease, and hunger afflicted soldiers and civilians alike. With an estimated total of 750,000 fatalities over the four years, it remains the United States' most costly war.

◀ This photograph of Union soldiers was taken by Mathew Brady, who shot over 10,000 images during the conflict, showing the reality rather than the romanticization of war. For this reason Brady is held to be the "father of photojournalism."

FIGHT TO THE DEATH

When war broke out between the northern and southern states in the spring of 1861, most soldiers did not expect a prolonged conflict, especially given the North's material and manpower advantages. Yet it took four bloody years to bring about a victory and a resolution.

The American Civil War was, in many ways, a conflict between two ways of life. The northern United States was (generalizing significantly) urbanized and industrialized, with high birth rates and massive European immigration. It was also ideologically opposed to the practice of slavery, although racism still ran deep. The South, by contrast, felt itself to be agrarian and traditional, its massive plantation economy dependent on the practice of slavery, with a smaller population and lower birth rates.

The Civil War, precipitated by the election of antislavery President Abraham Lincoln and the retaliatory secession of Confederate states, brought these two ways of life into a violent clash that would eventually consume the lives of more than 750,000 citizens over a four-year period.

OPPOSING SIDES

At the beginning of the conflict, the advantages seemed largely stacked in favor of the North. It could mobilize up to 3 million men, as opposed to the 1 million of the Confederacy. It had a far more powerful navy, through which it could impose a deep blockade of the southern ports, and it controlled most of the major railroads to the west and south. It also had far greater industrial capacity, including military output of rifles, artillery pieces, and kit.

These inequalities were noticeable at the frontlines, particularly in terms of the quality and quantity of Confederate matériel, yet the South's fighting qualities and leadership more than compensated. In fact, about 30 percent of Union Army officers defected to the Confederacy in the opening months

ROBERT E. LEE

Robert E. Lee (1807–1870) was a truly talented commander. Before the war he served as a U.S. Army combat engineer and colonel, but defected to the Confederates in 1861. Tactically, Lee was an intelligent leader, often outmaneuvering Union forces. Strategically he was less circumspect.

▼ Soldiers of the 44th Indiana Infantry Regiment, 1863. As well as taking heavy casualties, the regiment lost over 200 men to disease.

▲ Artillery teams perform their drill in fortified defenses around Washington. The gun team commander stands to the right.

of the war, providing the South with a cadre of excellent and experienced leaders—men like Robert E. Lee and Thomas "Stonewall" Jackson.

NEW WAYS OF WAR

The American Civil War was a brutal conflict, with massive casualties incurred on both sides. The Battle of Shiloh, on April 6–7, 1862, for example, cost 13,000 Union and 11,000 Confederate lives, while the combined casualties of Gettysburg on July 1–3, 1863, reached over 50,000. The high casualties were partly the product of traditional linear infantry tactics meeting the new generations of accurate rifled muskets and improved artillery, which turned the packed ranks of men into standing targets. Professionalism was also limited among many enthusiastic but ill-trained militia and volunteer forces, who consequently made poor tactical judgments on unforgiving battlefields.

For such reasons, we see a shift toward emplaced defensive warfare in the later years of the war, as the South attempted to hold on against the rising

> "But **what a cruel thing is war**; to separate and **destroy families and friends,** and mar the purest joys and happiness."
>
> ROBERT E. LEE, LETTER TO HIS WIFE, DECEMBER 25, 1862

reality of defeat. We also see a new cruelty within the conflict. Civilians suffered terribly, both from the direct encounters with enemy soldiers and from the effects of huge armies foraging their supplies. The war ended in 1865, following a series of seminal Confederate defeats. Yet in some ways, the Civil War was a portent of the future World Wars in the 20th century.

▶ Ulysses S. Grant, seen here in a camp in Virginia, was a ruthless general, largely responsible for unleashing a punishing campaign of attrition against the South.

THE SOLDIERS OF THE NORTH

The Union Army was a rather chaotic organization, its manpower a mixture of former militia soldiers, virtually untrained volunteers, adventurers lured by cash incentives, plus a solid cadre of regular soldiers. Nevertheless, it was a war-winning force.

The two main sources of Union infantry were a relatively small regular army plus the broad and colorful variety of militia troops, essentially half-militarized civilians formed for the purpose of state defense. To this picture were added tens of thousands of volunteers, mostly young men from rural agricultural or urban industrial backgrounds, who flocked eagerly to the cause.

IN SERVICE

At the very outset of the war, in April 1861, Lincoln called for just 75,000 militiamen to serve for 90 days—that was the force and time deemed sufficient to quash the rebel forces in

◀ A group of Union officers in camp. In 1861–62 the quality of officers could be extremely poor, but from 1862 the standard of leadership generally began to improve.

the South. As the fighting escalated, however, it quickly became clear that this number would not do the job, so Lincoln opened the net wider with a three-year enlistment program. Later in the war, by which time the Union forces had suffered heavy losses, more men were scraped into service

DESERTION

Desertion was a problem for both sides during the Civil War. In March 1863, for example,125,000 soldiers were AWOL from the Union Army alone. The problem became worse as more men were drafted later in the war, even though the maximum penalty (rarely imposed) was death.

▼ A company of Union infantry wait to board a train. Rail logistics meant that soldiers could be deployed more rapidly around the battlefront.

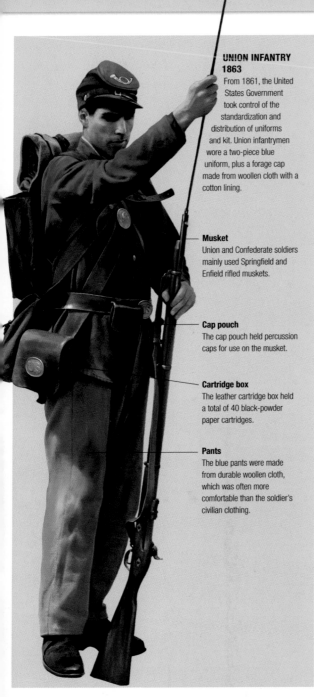

UNION INFANTRY 1863

From 1861, the United States Government took control of the standardization and distribution of uniforms and kit. Union infantrymen wore a two-piece blue uniform, plus a forage cap made from woollen cloth with a cotton lining.

Musket
Union and Confederate soldiers mainly used Springfield and Enfield rifled muskets.

Cap pouch
The cap pouch held percussion caps for use on the musket.

Cartridge box
The leather cartridge box held a total of 40 black-powder paper cartridges.

Pants
The blue pants were made from durable woollen cloth, which was often more comfortable than the soldier's civilian clothing.

▲ A cavalry orderly stands with his mount at Antietam, 1862. Cavalry became less centrally important to battlefield tactics during the war.

through a draft, with agents offering financial inducement, known somewhat disparagingly as "Bounty Men."

LIFE ON DUTY

The life of the Union infantryman was arduous and austere. Long periods were spent marching across the vast theater, carrying packs and equipment that weighed up to 50 pounds/23kg. Disease whittled down the ranks constantly, particularly dysentery and cholera. Leave was rare and for some the prospect held little appeal anyway, particularly if the war was raging across their hometowns and villages.

There was also the issue of discipline. The American soldier often came from traditions with a scant regard for authority, and many young and inexperienced officers struggled to maintain order and direction over the men. This situation, plus poor training and inexperienced leaders, contributed to some of the early Union defeats. Yet the Union soldiers could also show incredible pride toward their unit, and courage in battle.

THE SOLDIERS OF THE SOUTH

The soldiers of the Confederacy served and fought in privation. With the South suffering under the Union blockade, everything was in short supply, from food to weaponry. The Southern soldier was nevertheless a hardy warrior, stubborn in defense and ferocious in attack.

In much the same way as the Union Army, the Confederate Army was put together in a rather hasty and haphazard fashion during the early months of the war. A large part of the manpower was provided by militia troops, commanded by local dignitaries or influential citizens rather than professional officers. But sensing the depth of the impending crisis, in April 1862 the South introduced the draft, making all males between the ages of 18 and 35 liable for military service. Under the command of some former U.S. Army officers, many of these men grew into effective fighters, despite their often bedraggled appearance.

SHORTAGES

The critical challenge that faced the Confederate infantryman throughout the war was the shortages of supplies. Because of the Union control over shipping lanes and many of the

▲ A portrait of Confederate soldiers from Louisiana in 1861. Fiddlers were often the center of entertainment in the unit.

▼ Crude Confederate winter huts made from wood panels. Mud was packed between the logs to provide some basic insulation.

country's railroads, plus the South's limited industrial capability, everything was scarce—food, rifles, ammunition, uniforms, and field equipment. Thus the Confederate soldier was compelled to learn to live light, foraging off the land and constantly putting weaponry and equipment to maximum effective use.

EYEWITNESS ACCOUNT

"Tired and sleepy we still march on, and as we come in proximity of the battle ground the scores of wounded passing to the rear remind us that bloody work is going on. A little farther on, to the left of the pike, we halt & 'load at will.' No sooner done, then in again. The enemy's batteries give us shot & shell in abundance causing many muscular contractions in the spinal column of our line."
—James J. Fitzpatrick, 16th Mississippi Infantry

"Battle, **oh horrid battle**. What sights I have seen, now see around me. **I am Wounded!**"

SGT. JONATHAN STOWE

Confederate troops took as much as they could from the dead and captured Union forces, including boots and personal effects, to supplement their official kit.

BELIEF AND BELONGING

Despite the perilous nature of their supply situation, Confederate infantry constantly impressed both their leaders and their enemies with their willingness to fight. Largely this is explained by their intense motivation. Most Confederate soldiers saw the war in terms of protecting a traditional, God-fearing lifestyle that they felt running through their veins. To this day, many Southern Americans still refuse to refer to the "Civil War," but rather to the "War of Northern Aggression." Union soldiers grew to fear the "rebel yell," the chilling scream the gray-clad soldiers unleashed when they left their positions to go on the attack.

When not conducting operations, the daily life of the Confederate soldier would be much like that of his Northern counterpart—woken around 5 a.m. to the sound of drums, then a quick breakfast before an endless round of camp and fatigue duties. These tasks would include gathering firewood, cleaning weapons and kit, digging defenses, collecting water, feeding/grooming horses, plus the tedium of hours of guard duty. But given purpose, the Confederate infantryman was a dependable trooper.

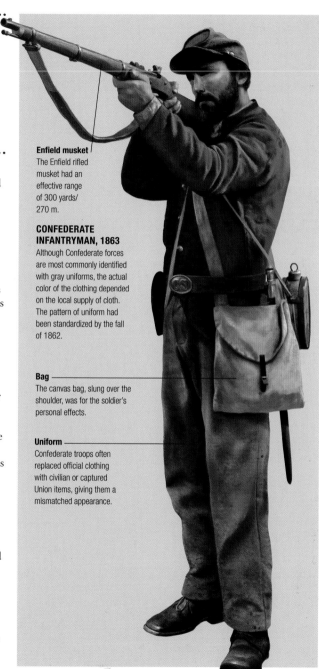

Enfield musket
The Enfield rifled musket had an effective range of 300 yards/ 270 m.

CONFEDERATE INFANTRYMAN, 1863
Although Confederate forces are most commonly identified with gray uniforms, the actual color of the clothing depended on the local supply of cloth. The pattern of uniform had been standardized by the fall of 1862.

Bag
The canvas bag, slung over the shoulder, was for the soldier's personal effects.

Uniform
Confederate troops often replaced official clothing with civilian or captured Union items, giving them a mismatched appearance.

THE RISE OF THE ENGINEER

Military engineers were few in number at the beginning of the Civil War. Within weeks, however, it became apparent that these uniquely skilled individuals were going to be critical to the developing conflict, and their numbers and roles expanded rapidly.

Insight into the value of the engineer during the Civil War is given, with feeling, in the following quotation from a Union infantry veteran: "They... became fast friends and companions. They excelled [sic] a gymnasium for the development of chest and muscle; they sheltered us from the rain and the sun; they hid us from the foe; they carried our wounded, and received our dead. When as veterans with discharges in our pockets, we took our last look at the camp, our eyes lingered longest where the old arks were parked, battered and plugged but fitted and equipped, ready for another move." As this soldier suggests, engineers were not just specialists called on to perform abstract technical challenges, but were central to the very life and morale of the army.

▲ The artillery battery at Fort Brady, Petersburg. Note the intensive landscaping required to create the protective emplacements.

▼ The footlocker of a U.S. Army Engineer officer of the Civil War. The contents are: 1 footlocker box; 2 U.S. Army Engineers insignia; 3 shaving razor; 4 shaving pouch; 5 shaving brush; 6 hair brush; 7 tape measure box; 8 tape measure; 9 comb; 10 coin purse; 11 accessory box; 12 grapeshot round; 13 miniature silk United States flag; 14 another coin purse; 15 newspaper cuttings; 16 wire measure; 17 leather sword belt.

EXPANSION

At the beginning of the Civil War, military engineers were in short supply in both Union and Confederate forces. In the Union Army there were just 43 professional engineering personnel in January 1861. By the end of the year, in contrast, there were two volunteer regiments and a regular Engineer Battalion, overseen by the Corps of Engineers. The Confederate Corps of Engineers was established in 1861, manned by officers dedicated to providing combat engineering services, but only in May 1863 did it expand as an enlisted branch. There were never really enough engineers, on either side, but what they lacked in manpower they more than made up for with ingenuity, often from civilians experienced in engineering trades.

ROLES

The roles of the engineers were broad and challenging, and were added on top of standard infantry training. The engineer also received training in

> "The company was turned out at **2 o'clock in the morning** to **unload the Pontoons** which then arrived."
>
> NEWTON HARTSHORN, ENGINEER, 1862

artillery theory and handling. A very specific role was that of "pontooneer," responsible for creating bridges over the hundreds of waterways that laced the theater. For example, in just nine hours on February 26, 1862, Union engineers put up a pontoon bridge 830 feet/253 m long across the Potomac River; support for the bridge structure was ingeniously provided by a total of 41 boats.

Engineers also developed static defenses, including the prodigious Union defensive works around

▲ Union engineers create a pontoon bridge, consisting of a wooden platform laid and stabilized across a series of boats.

▼ Engineers, here seen in a crude shelter in Virginia in 1864, also laid the infrastructure for telegraph communications.

Washington D.C., which by 1864 included 68 forts, 100 artillery batteries, and 20 miles/32 km of trenches. In addition, engineers built railroads, created camps, dug mines, laid roads, maintained lighthouses and port facilities, mapped out territories, and generally oiled the wheels of the war.

PERSONAL FIREPOWER

The Civil War was fought during an important period of transition in the history of firearms. The sun was setting on the days of the old smoothbore musket, but was rising over a new era in breechloading repeaters.

The principal weapon of the vast majority of soldiers during the Civil War was the muzzle-loading single-shot musket, much like those that had been carried by the soldiers of the Napoleonic Wars. Yet there were some crucial differences from the weapons of that earlier conflict.

First, the Civil War was fought in the percussion era. Gone were the flintlock mechanisms of the past (although some were still seen in the hands of irregulars), replaced by explosive percussion caps placed under the gun's hammer, on a nipple with a vent connecting it to the main chamber. The percussion lock was quicker to use than a flintlock, and it gave more reliable ignition. Each soldier carried a tin of caps at the ready as part of his kit.

▲ Some of the firepower and kit carried by a regular infantryman. 1 Colt Model 1851 Navy revolver; 2 tin of percussion caps; 3 gunpowder flask; 4 bullet screw; 5 bullet mold; 6 musket tool; 7 cleaning rod sections.

RIFLED ARMS

Smoothbore muskets were still used in large numbers during the Civil War, but the weight of fire was now delivered by rifled weapons. Rifles, through imparting gyroscopic spin to the projectile, had greatly improved accuracy and range, meaning a soldier could aim at and hit a human-sized target hundreds of yards away. The accuracy was enhanced by the French-developed Minié bullet, a special bullet that could be loaded easily into the barrel but which expanded on firing to engage firmly with the rifling.

The rifled arms most familiar to both sides were the .58-caliber Springfield and the British-imported .577-caliber Enfield. To fire either weapon, the soldier first retrieved a paper cartridge from his cartridge box. The cartridge contained both powder and ball, and the soldier tore the top off the cartridge with his teeth, tipped the powder into the muzzle, then rammed the ball and paper down the muzzle with the ramrod, seating them firmly.

◄ Bayoneted rifles on racks at the arsenal of the 134th Illinois Volunteer Infantry. Bayonets were mainly used for charges against fixed positions.

Then he half-cocked the hammer, placed a percussion cap on the nipple and fully cocked the hammer. Only now would he be able to aim and fire the weapon. Each soldier was issued with somewhere between 60 and 80 cartridges, with the cartridge box holding 40 ready rounds.

REPEATERS
Supplementing the muzzle-loading firearms, the Civil War also saw the introduction of new generations of repeating firearms. Cavalry troops, for example, warmed to the Sharps carbine, a breechloading weapon that still used paper cartridges, but mechanically upped the rate of fire to about 5rpm.

Far more revolutionary were the new weapons that fired unitary metallic cartridges. The Spencer repeating rifle, manufactured in the United States and personally endorsed by President Lincoln, for example, held seven shots in a tubular magazine in the stock, and the cartridges were fed through the gun via a lever action. A soldier with a Spencer could fire up to 20 accurate rounds every minute. Most of the 94,000 Spencers were in Union hands,

▲ This scene from the Battle of Shiloh, Tennessee, April 6–7, 1862, shows the full spectrum of firepower, from rifles up to field artillery.

▼ Cavalry soldiers were armed with carbines (shortened rifles) but also relied on the traditional saber for close-quarter fighting.

and they inflicted terrible casualties on Confederate ranks, more used to the rhythms of muzzle-loaders. Other landmark repeating weapons, although used in very small numbers, were the 16-shot Henry rifle and also some of the earliest examples of the Gatling hand-cranked machine gun.

SHARPSHOOTERS

Sharpshooters were the forerunners of snipers. They were light infantry trained in the art of accurate shooting over long distances, and in fighting with flexible tactics to outwit opponents and inflict attrition on a less flexible enemy.

Although many American soldiers were competent rifle shots on account of the country's strong hunting traditions, the vast majority had only the most basic shooting skills.

BERDAN'S SHARPSHOOTERS

One man with a little more vision was Hiram G. Berdan, an engineer and inventor who also happened to be a superb shot with a rifle. In the summer of 1861, wanting to make a more seminal contribution to the Union war effort, Berdan proposed to the government that he form and train an elite force of riflemen, each a crack shot and armed with the best weaponry. His

▼ The Union sharpshooter "California Joe" (real name Truman Head) with his Sharps rifle, 1862. When he joined up he was 52 years old, having lied about his age, but he proved to be an astonishingly good shot.

EYEWITNESS ACCOUNT

"We waited a long time for a sight at him but he did not show himself. It was getting toward night, when a puff of smoke was seen to rise from a tree near the fort, and a bullet came whistling past our heads. We now arranged our plans. By the aid of a glass I could see his black 'mug' peeping from behind a tree. I elevated my sight and fired. It must have come close, for he sprang out. As he did so Brown fired, and 'my joker' fell, with a bullet through him. Brown had his sight elevated for fifteen hundred yards!"
—A member of the 1st U.S.S.S., describing the killing of a rebel sharpshooter

▲ A recruiting poster for sharpshooters in the state of Pennsylvania. The sharpshooters were inundated with volunteers, but many failed to pass the initial shooting tests.

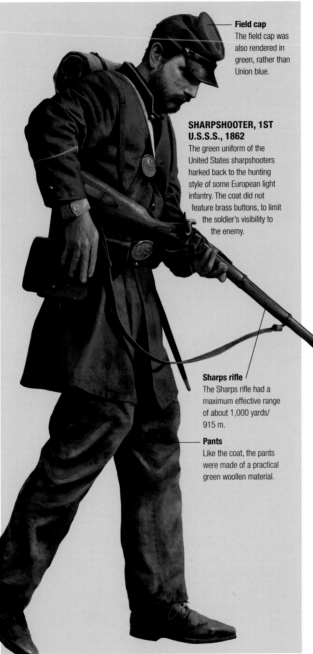

Field cap
The field cap was also rendered in green, rather than Union blue.

SHARPSHOOTER, 1ST U.S.S.S., 1862
The green uniform of the United States sharpshooters harked back to the hunting style of some European light infantry. The coat did not feature brass buttons, to limit the soldier's visibility to the enemy.

Sharps rifle
The Sharps rifle had a maximum effective range of about 1,000 yards/ 915 m.

Pants
Like the coat, the pants were made of a practical green woollen material.

"By our dress **we were known far and wide**, and the appellation of '**Green Coats**' was soon acquired."

CAPTAIN C.A. STEVENS

proposition was accepted and he started gathering individuals for what would become the 1st and 2nd Regiments of United States Sharpshooters.

CRACK SHOTS
The men who became sharpshooters were volunteers, but only men who could shoot well in the first place were accepted. Each man had to pass a test in which he put ten consecutive shots into a 10 inch/25 cm circle at 200 yards/182 m. Once in the ranks, the soldier was given further exhaustive training in shooting with the formidable Sharps breechloading rifle, enabling him to strike targets at ranges of hundreds of yards, especially if the rifle was equipped with one of the early variants of the telescopic sight.

The sharpshooters became the scourge of the Confederate forces. They dressed in green as an early form of camouflage, and preferred covert movement to open warfare. They were skilled at living light, traveling with limited kit and foraging off the land. Their targets were those enemy individuals who had skill and leadership; in other words, the people who would be hardest for the enemy to replace. Confederate officers were natural targets, but so too were engineers and artillerymen. Their presence taught the enemy valuable lessons about cover.

of a soldier, leisure time away from the frontline is one of the most precious commodities there is. The use of that spare time depends upon a multitude of variables, from the theater to which the soldier is deployed to the amount of spare time given.

The importance of morale in any army should not be underestimated. Morale is fostered and maintained by a complex series of cultural and practical phenomena—good leadership, belief in a cause, unit pride, high-quality training and equipment, food and logistics, and so on But a timeless ingredient of morale is one of the simplest—time off to rest, recuperate, and have fun.

FINDING THE MOMENTS
Giving the soldier time off duty is not simply an indulgence, but actually has a critical role to play in the soldier's long-term performance. During World War II, studies into the onset of combat stress in Allied soldiers found that sending a fatigued soldier back behind the line for just a single day, to get hot food, a change of clothes, and a bit of extra sleep, could make the difference between psychological collapse and

▲ American troops play music in their camp during the Spanish–American War, 1898. In the days before recorded music, armies often had a high number of musicians.

continuing endurance. Armies that neglect off-duty rest or leave tend to have appalling levels of morale, such as experienced by Russian soldiers in World War I.

PURSUITS
Prior to the 20th century, a soldier's off-duty hours would generally be spent within his barracks, playing card games, board games, music and engaging in low-level gambling. In Roman times, for example, soldiers might be found playing *latrunculi*, which was similar to modern chess or checkers. Sport has also always been popular, whether 19th-century British officers indulging in a polo match or the rank and file kicking a football around.

Such pursuits continue to this day, but in the 20th century entertainment

◀ Sport has always formed a cornerstone of off-duty entertainiment. Here a post-World War I British boxing team proudly displays its achievements

▲ Anzac troops visit the Sphinx in Egypt while off duty, 1940. A foreign deployment was often the greatest chance a soldier had of seeing the wider world.

for troops became increasingly organized. This was partly to maintain morale, but was also an attempt to keep soldiers out of trouble with prostitutes and alcohol. For example, in World War I the Young Men's Christian Association (YMCA) established no fewer than 250 recreation centers for troops in the United Kingdom and dozens more in France and Belgium. One such center at Étaples, France, served 200,000 cups of cocoa every month.

Soldiers also increasingly spent off-duty hours watching movies or shows provided by military entertainment organizations. In 1941, the United Services Organization (USO) was formed in America, and throughout World War II put on shows for soldiers across all theaters, often involving stars of the time. Of course,

the ultimate off-duty status was to be on leave, from a short weekend pass through to a whole month off, the latter typically given to soldiers who had been through sustained periods of combat.

► A group of American soldiers entertain themselves with a barrack-room dice game in France during or shortly after World War I.

FOOD AND LIVING CONDITIONS

Camp life was a basic affair for both sides during the American Civil War. Life in the field was spent under canvas or in rudimentary wood-and-mud huts during the winter months, and food tended to be repetitious and was often scarce.

As a general rule, Union troops tended to be better quartered than Confederate soldiers, thanks to the industrial resources of the North. In fact, Confederates were often reliant on captured Union stocks of tents and camp equipment, making their camps much less standardized than those of their opponents.

CAMP CONSTRUCTION

The nature of the camp depended on the season in which it was built. During spring and summer months—the seasons typically reserved for the most vigorous campaigning—forces lived in tents of various designs. Each Union soldier was issued with a "dog tent," essentially a piece of canvas that could be thrown over a pole or cord to provide crude shelter. Larger and more enclosed tents were developed to house 5–6 men, and both sides used the conical

Sibley tent, which stood 12 feet/3m tall on a central pole and had a diameter of 18 feet/5.5 m.

Life within the tents was not pleasant. The interiors quickly became dirty and damaged, and torn canvas meant occupants and equipment were exposed to

▲ A sutler's store, with large numbers of soldiers gathered outside. The sutler was a civilian who supplied food, clothing, and other items to an army, often following the force on its campaign.

▲ Everyday kit: 1 hardtack biscuits, tasteless but sufficient to ward off hunger; 2 water pitcher; 3 sewing kit, for minor uniform repairs.

◄ A particularly well-constructed Union tent. Two bunks are set up inside, plus a small table for writing letters. The footlockers at the base of each bunk and the quality of the accommodation indicate that this is likely a tent for officers. A wooden case outside the tent provided further storage and a basic dining table.

the elements. During the winter, the soldiers went into more permanent and substantial winter quarters. These were basically log huts constructed from local materials, covered with mud to block the air gaps and increase insulation. Roofs were made from tent canvas or wooden boards, and each hut featured a fireplace and chimney, plus some uncomfortable wooden bunks for the occupants.

FOOD

Civil War soldiers spent much of their lives thinking about food, either its quantity or quality. In the Union Army, soldiers were issued with three-day rations, which were generally composed of salt pork (occasionally there was fresh beef), "hardtack" flour biscuits, rice, peas, beans, potatoes, and salt. Coffee beans were also issued as a luxury; the soldiers would roast and grind the beans themselves in the field.

For Confederate troops, the diet was more restrictive, typically bacon, molasses, peas, and rice, plus whatever vegetables could be foraged. However,

▲ This scene perfectly illustrates the austere nature of camp life. The trees on the right have likely been hacked down to provide materials for the huts. One soldier is washing his clothes, although this was often done by a camp laundress.

▼ A cook presides over dinner for musicians of the 3rd New Hampshire Regiment in South Carolina. Note how young the boy on the right is—about 20 percent of Civil War soldiers were under 18.

on both sides the lack of fresh fruit and vegetables, particularly in the latter years of the war, resulted in scurvy affecting up to 3 percent of soldiers within particular units. Furthermore, with so many men packed into a large camp, diseases such as measles, smallpox and dysentery ran quickly through a camp, often causing more casualties than actual combat. Camp life in the Civil War was not by any means easy living.

AFRICAN-AMERICAN SOLDIERS

African-Americans served on both sides during the Civil War, although naturally in far greater numbers for the North. Yet even though the war was fought largely over the issue of slavery, black soldiers in the Union forces also suffered from racism and discrimination.

For the Union, African-Americans provided a large source of manpower not readily available to the slave-owning South. And yet, at the beginning of the war a federal statute dating back to 1792 prevented black soldiers from serving in the armed forces. This was only fully repealed late in 1862, and the following year the Bureau of Colored Troops was established to oversee the recruitment of African-Americans into Union forces.

UNION SERVICE

The numbers of African-Americans who joined the Union forces were significant—179,000 men in the army alone, which constituted roughly 10 percent of the entire Union Army. (Another 19,000 served in the U.S. Navy.) Some 160 units were manned wholly or partly by African-Americans, and in combat many of those units showed conspicuous bravery. The 54th

▲ African-American soldiers aim their rifles. Units of black soldiers were led by white officers, so training levels could be poor.

▼ Buglers of the 22nd and 10th Cavalry Regiments. As well as musicians, African-Americans also served as color bearers.

Regiment of Massachusetts Volunteers, for example, suffered 75 percent casualties for their dogged assault on Fort Wagner in July 1863.

Yet the majority of African-Americans did not see frontline combat. The North was itself deeply imbued with racism, and most black soldiers were kept segregated and in labor and support roles. Furthermore, black soldiers were paid $10 per month but with a $3 clothing deduction, while white soldiers in the same roles received $13 and no clothing deduction. This situation was finally

> "If **slaves** will make **good soldiers** [then] our whole **theory of slavery is wrong**."
>
> CONFEDERATE COLONEL HOWELL
> COBB, GEORGIA

▲ A portrait of "Drummer" Jackson, a former slave serving as a drummer in the 79th United States Colored Troops during the Civil War.

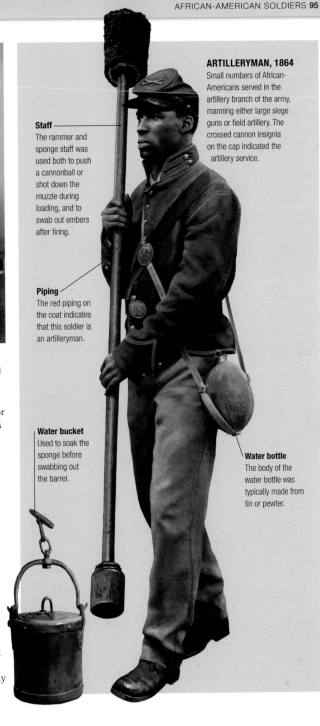

ARTILLERYMAN, 1864
Small numbers of African-Americans served in the artillery branch of the army, manning either large siege guns or field artillery. The crossed cannon insignia on the cap indicated the artillery service.

Staff
The rammer and sponge staff was used both to push a cannonball or shot down the muzzle during loading, and to swab out embers after firing.

Piping
The red piping on the coat indicates that this soldier is an artilleryman.

Water bucket
Used to soak the sponge before swabbing out the barrel.

Water bottle
The body of the water bottle was typically made from tin or pewter.

overturned in June 1864, and the lost pay was retroactively instated. The poor conditions in which African-Americans were kept is perhaps indicated by the fact that 40,000 died in the war, but 30,000 of that number succumbed to disease, not to combat.

CONFEDERATE SERVICE
Black soldiers did serve in the Confederate forces, but almost exclusively as slave labor supporting the field armies. It was not uncommon for Confederate officers to bring with them a small retinue of familiar slaves from their plantations, who would look after their owner on campaign, cooking and cleaning and attending to personal effects. In March 1865, the Confederacy passed a law allowing freed black men to enlist with the permission of their employers; naturally few men actually did so.

THE EXPERIENCE OF BATTLE

The flying banners and stirring speeches of commanders could do nothing to mask the horror of combat on the Civil War battlefields. Amid clouds of gunpowder smoke, individual soldiers fought with desperation in an attempt to survive the day.

It must be remembered that about three-quarters of a soldier's day-to-day existence in the Civil War would have been spent doing very little, just waiting for something purposeful to happen. Yet periodically, soldiers would be immersed in the experience of a major battle, an astonishing and visceral spectacle of firepower, sharpened steel, and violence that many of them would not survive.

BATTLEFIELD CHAOS

Although battle experience changed depending on the particular engagement, there were some constants. One of the greatest challenges for officers was keeping some form of coherence in their units. During an assault, soldiers would have to advance across rough, shot-blasted ground, men being felled constantly by musket balls and blown apart by artillery shot, while attempting to maintain ranks and delivery of coherent volley fire.

Officers would attempt to control the effort, but their presence would often be lost in noise and choking clouds of gunpowder smoke, and of

▲ Reenactors seek to portray something of the chaos of the Battle of Gettysburg. Bodies littered the battlefield for many weeks after the engagement.

course they were also just as likely to be killed themselves. The battle might therefore degenerate into a desperate and individualistic scrap, with individuals or small groups fighting almost independently of one another. This problem could be made worse by difficult terrain, such as forested areas.

▼ Here we see a Springfield Model 1861 musket, one of the defining weapons of the conflict, set beside three forms of Civil War grenade. Most interesting is the "Ketchum Grenade" (4), which was fin-stabilized and detonated on impact by a percussion cap in the nose.

> " ...the **dead and wounded** men were literally **piled there in heaps.** "
>
> EYEWITNESS TO ANTIETAM

▲ The outer line of the Confederate fortifications in front of Petersburg, Virginia. The bank of earth provided protection from enemy shot and bullets.

An example of such chaos can be seen in the Battle of the Crater on July 30, 1864, fought as part of the Siege of Petersburg. Union forces detonated 320 kegs of gunpowder in a mine beneath the Confederate lines, killing 278 enemy soldiers. They then fatally delayed the advance against a stunned opponent, meaning hundreds of Union men became trapped in the crater, where they were massacred by Confederates firing from the rim. The Union took 3,798 casualties, and many African-American troops captured by the Confederates were bayoneted.

▲ A highly decorated Civil War drum. Drummers were generally unarmed on the battlefield.

▲ Like drums, bugles were used to issue battlefield commands, although their sound was often lost in the din of battle.

▶ A roll of surgical instruments. The war ushered in many medical innovations in the field, such as better treatments for chest wounds and faster, more efficient amputations.

MUSIC IN BATTLE

On the Civil War battlefield, musicians (when they weren't being used as surgeons' assistants) might play entire tunes to stir men to action. Popular tunes were "The Battle Cry of Freedom" (Union) and "I wish I was in Dixie" (Confederate).

WOUNDED

It was the fate of hundreds of thousands of soldiers to be seriously wounded on the battlefields of the war. At first, medical provision was extremely poor in coping with large numbers of casualties. It was gradually improved, however, especially in the Union Army with the introduction of caravans of horse-drawn ambulances to take casualties to field hospitals.

The hospitals could be nightmarish places. Dead and dying often lay side by side, and piles of amputated limbs were stacked up by the sides of surgeons' tents. Efficiencies in surgical technique, however, meant it took a trained doctor only six minutes to remove a limb.

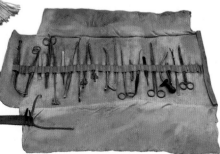

> "On the frontier, **in the clear light of the morning**, when the mountain side is dotted with smoke puffs...**every ridge sparkles with bright sword blade**s."
>
> WINSTON CHURCHILL, INDIAN NORTHWEST FRONTIER, 1897

COLONIAL WARS

1850–1914

European troops deployed to colonies in the Americas, Asia, or Africa often had extraordinary experiences in equally extraordinary places. Some soldiers might spend their entire adult lives in tropical India or deepest Africa, learning to live with the climate and being periodically called on to fight brutal colonial wars.

◄ Soldiers of the City Imperial Volunteers Regiment march from Paddington Station, London, to a thanksgiving service at St. Paul's Cathedral on October 29, 1900, as they return from fighting in South Africa during the Boer War.

STRANGE NEW WORLD

The global political map of the 19th century was colored heavily by colonialism. European powers—especially Britain, Germany, Portugal, Spain, and France—had taken chunks of the wider world for themselves, and needed soldiers to maintain restless territories.

The 18th and 19th centuries were times of intense colonial expansion, as the European powers fell over themselves in a military and cultural landgrab. Many of these takeovers were wrapped in the language of Christian benevolence, but in reality were simply imperial and commercial aggression, delivered and accomplished, more often than not, at the point of the gun.

GLOBAL COLONIES

Looking back at the maps of this period, we are struck by how much of the world was under colonial authority. By far the largest of the empires was that created by Britain. By the end of the 19th century, the sun literally never set on the British Empire, which had colonies including Canada, Nigeria, Sudan, Rhodesia, South Africa, the Indian subcontinent, Burma, Malaya, Borneo, Australia, and New Zealand. But Britain was far from alone on the imperial stage. Africa was arbitrarily divided between France

▲ African men suspected of spying are interrogated by British troops in 1899 in South Africa.

▼ An idealized portrait of Lieutenants Melvill and Coghill dying in their attempt to save the Queen's colors at the Battle of Isandlwana, January 22, 1879, in the Anglo–Zulu War.

(which occupied most of northwest Africa), Italy, Germany, Portugal, and Belgium. The Dutch and Germans also controlled significant territories in East Asia. Europeans were not the only colonizers, however. The Ottoman Empire, for instance, wrapped itself around much of the Middle East, and in the early 20th century the Japanese acquired the Korean Peninsula and many Pacific territories.

CONTROLLING THE COLONIES

Acquiring the colonies in the first place was no easy matter, and they often had to be claimed by force against spirited resistance. Major British wars generated by colonial expansion include the Anglo–Zulu War of 1879 and the Boer Wars of 1880–81 and 1899–1902.

Yet taking over a region was only the beginning of a long story. Controlling and administrating the colony was an entirely different, and long-term,

challenge. This was partly accomplished by imposing a new civil service, typically based on European models of government, but also by stationing permanent large bodies of troops throughout the territories.

Colonial postings were a learning experience for a whole generation of

> ## "At night we could not sleep, what with the heat and the noise the jackals made."
>
> JOHN PEARMAN, BRITISH SOLDIER,
> INDIA, OCTOBER 1845

European soldiers. Differences between the soldiers' countries of origin and the colonized nations were often profound. Everything was different—language, law, religion, clothing, climate, flora and fauna, cultural practices, diseases, diets, and sexual relations. Some of the more enlightened soldiers, especially officers, adapted to a new way of life, learning the local language and customs and attempting to build bridges between colonizers and colonized. Countless others, however, simply attempted to recreate their own cultures in a new context, or impose foreign values on the locals. Sometimes the two peoples came to understand one another, but often friction boiled over into conflict, such as in the Indian Mutiny of 1857, resulting in atrocity and counteratrocity.

▲ In a painting tellingly entitled *A friendly power in Egypt* by W.C. Horsley, the 41st (Welch) Regiment marches imperiously through Cairo's Metwali Gate, 1887.

LANGUAGE SKILLS

Soldiers who learned the local language tended to be officers who had received classical language training (Greek and Latin) at university. Language guides were invaluable, such as *Hobson-Jobson, an Anglo-Indian Dictionary*, by Henry Yule and Arthur C. Burnell (1886).

EUROPEAN FORCES IN AFRICA

Africa was an exotic posting for any European regiment. Yet, as the soldiers quickly discovered, the conditions they experienced there could be especially challenging and unforgiving, and many men would never see their home countries again.

Whether reflecting on the British in South Africa, the Germans in East Africa, or the Belgians in the Congo, some experiences united all soldiers deployed to African lands.

SURVIVAL ESSENTIALS

For most of the year, apart from when torrential seasonal rains arrived, the soldiers in 19th-century Africa labored under terrible heat, in uniforms better suited to temperate European climates. This meant drinking copious amounts of water to stay hydrated, but finding clean supplies of water was a problem. Soldiers tended to extract water from whatever sources they found, as long as they were not visibly polluted by dead animals. In many cases even apparently clean water was not safe to drink, yet

> "They came on **most determinedly**... They drove our fellows out of the Hospital, **killed the patients.**"
>
> BRITISH OFFICER WALTER DUNNE, WHO FOUGHT AT RORKE'S DRIFT, 1879

▼ The Battle of Rorke's Drift on January 22–23, 1879, saw 150 British and allied native troops fight off an army of 3,000–4,000 Zulu warriors in a harrowing clash.

EYEWITNESS ACCOUNT

"It is almost impossible to get an accurate return of food, but I think we must have over three weeks' supply, the cattle, however, may be swept away at any moment, as of course they have to be kept in the wagon laager outside. I am keeping a small reserve in the ditches, where we stable the horses also, although the ground is perfectly open round here, except one or two small patches of wood, which would give cover, but which are being cut down..."
—Letter from Colonel Charles Pearson at Rorke's Drift, 1879

▲ British soldiers are transported aboard a troop ship to the Transvaal during the Boer War, their equipment hanging from the ship's rafters.

was used to fill up water canteens, the result being the rapid spread of cholera and other diseases. Meat came from either herds of cattle driven along with the units, or from less familiar bush sources—a battalion of soldiers passing through an area would typically have a terrible impact on local wildlife, both from hunting for food and killing for sport. For officers, big-game hunting was a highlight of Africa. Because of the heat, soldiers often slept on the ground in the open, the hard surface leading to many arthritic complaints.

BATTLE

Europeans in Africa faced diverse enemies. During the Boer War, for example, the British struggled against tough and hardy Boers, who were proficient shots and talented riders. During the Zulu War, by contrast, the British were challenged by a massive army of native warriors, armed with spears, clubs, and shields. Soldiers on all sides seemed periodically disposed to commit atrocities on their opponents. Capture by the Zulus was a special terror for all British, following the massacre at Isandlwana in 1879.

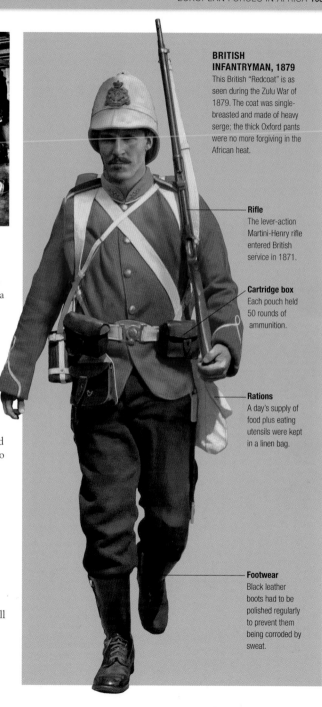

BRITISH INFANTRYMAN, 1879
This British "Redcoat" is as seen during the Zulu War of 1879. The coat was single-breasted and made of heavy serge; the thick Oxford pants were no more forgiving in the African heat.

Rifle
The lever-action Martini-Henry rifle entered British service in 1871.

Cartridge box
Each pouch held 50 rounds of ammunition.

Rations
A day's supply of food plus eating utensils were kept in a linen bag.

Footwear
Black leather boots had to be polished regularly to prevent them being corroded by sweat.

THE BRITISH IN INDIA

The British were the ruling presence in India from the mid-1700s until the country gained independence in 1947. The soldiers posted there in the second half of the 19th century attempted to create a familiar anglicized environment, with varying degrees of success.

The climate and weather were constant challenges for all those soldiers in service in India. As in Africa, the heat and humidity were exhausting and dangerous, even under shelter. One measure British troops used in camp was to dig a cooling pit into the earth floor beneath their tents, hang a wet sheet over the hole, then sit naked in the bottom, allowing the shade and evaporation to cool them down. The only time the climate became truly cool was during the monsoon season, although troops deployed to the Northwest Frontier could experience fiercely cold conditions during the winter months.

CULTURE SHOCK

For soldiers from parochial existences in Britain, the cultural and living conditions of India often came as something of a shock. In contact with the indigenous peoples, that shock

could cut both ways. Cities such as Calcutta teemed with lethal poverty, filth, violence, and vice, but the men would also have their crude racial stereotyping challenged by some of India's exceptionally well-educated middle and upper classes.

▲ An injured British soldier lies on the ground in Waziristan, in the much-troubled Northwest Frontier.

▼ A camel cart in India. British troops tended to have a low tolerance for camels, dismissing them as stubborn and aggressive.

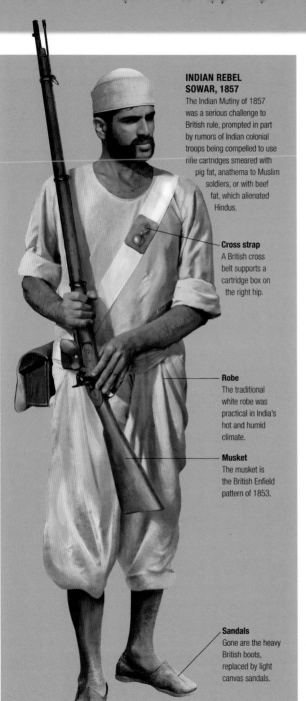

INDIAN REBEL SOWAR, 1857

The Indian Mutiny of 1857 was a serious challenge to British rule, prompted in part by rumors of Indian colonial troops being compelled to use rifle cartridges smeared with pig fat, anathema to Muslim soldiers, or with beef fat, which alienated Hindus.

Cross strap
A British cross belt supports a cartridge box on the right hip.

Robe
The traditional white robe was practical in India's hot and humid climate.

Musket
The musket is the British Enfield pattern of 1853.

Sandals
Gone are the heavy British boots, replaced by light canvas sandals.

For transportation and logistics, the British troops relied not only on familiar horses and mules, but also, less happily, on elephants and camels. India's expanding railroad network meant that by the end of the 19th century epic marches between strategic points became less common.

LUXURIOUS LIVING

On long operations into the Indian wilderness, British soldiers lived under canvas as they had done for centuries. Officers often had to buy their own tents, an unexpected and unwelcome cost for new arrivals in the country. Around the permanent bases, however, highly sophisticated British cantonments came into being. Officers and their families tended to live in modern developments of single-storied bungalows, framed by hedges and neat fences. These personnel were attended by legions of servants, performing every conceivable duty from cooking and cleaning to sprinkling water on the roof to cool the building. Unmarried officers tended to live communally in similar bungalows. Barracks for privates and NCOs (plus families) were far less salubrious and unsanitary, and disease proliferated there.

▼ Two British soldiers practice bayonet drill in India in the early 20th century. These drills would often come in handy when policing street crowd disturbances.

DISEASE, HEALTH, AND HYGIENE

It is hard to overstate the profound effect that disease had on soldiers during the colonial era. Sent to far-off, frequently tropical climes, European soldiers encountered a lethal range of untreatable diseases that carried them off in their thousands.

Despite its many improvements in public health, the 19th century was an era of disease. For European soldiers, sickness was even predatory within their home barracks, especially blights such as tuberculosis, cholera, and influenza. Barracks, often airless and with poor sanitation, tended to be perfect breeding grounds for disease. In 1852, the British physician Sir John Pringle publicly argued for barracks to have improved ventilation and the provision of well-maintained external latrines. Five years later, a British Royal Sanitary Commission studied the reasons why up to 17.5 percent of men in the tropics died in barracks

▲ British soldiers resting at a camp during the Boer War. Adequate rest was, and remains, a critical factor in maintaining health on operations.

▼ This horse-drawn hospital cart, with an Indian driver, was used to transport wounded British soldiers in South Africa during the Boer War.

"...undue importance is very often attached to impure water as a primary source of disease."

S. CLARK, PRACTICAL OBSERVATIONS ON THE HYGIENE OF THE ARMY IN INDIA, 1864

▲ A selection of 19th-century prosthetic limbs: 1 full leg prosthesis; 2 artificial hand; 3 prosthesis to replace the lower arm, with a hook fitting.

from disease. Their findings led to basic improvements, such as defining a minimum space required for each man, and the death rate fell to 9.5 percent.

TROPICAL TOLL

In the tropical colonies of Africa and Asia, mortality from disease remained devastating. Disease was by far the biggest killer. French forces in Madagascar in 1895, for example, suffered 19 combat losses but 4,000 deaths from malaria alone. Spain took 200,000 disease casualties in Cuba from 1868–78. The Germans suffered similarly in Africa and their Asian colonies. Other tropical maladies included yellow fever, dengue fever, and typhus, plus the ever-present issue of venereal disease.

Although cures for tropical diseases remained rare in the 19th century, soldiers would take certain preventative measures. With the connection between

malaria and mosquitoes established, for example, army engineers found that draining or avoiding local swamps reduced the incidences of infection. Many European forces in Africa and Asia began using quinine, which remained the standard antimalarial medication until the 1940s.

PREVENTION

The late 19th century saw an increase in the number of hygiene manuals issued to European soldiers in the colonies. Some provided good advice about diet, sanitation, and personal hygiene, although other theories had rather less scientific content. It was common for European soldiers to wear a "cholera belt," for example, a long strip of flannel or wool about 6 inches/15 cm deep, which was wrapped around the abdomen several times in the belief that it protected against the "chilling of the abdomen," which, it was believed, exposed the soldier to cholera. This senseless item persisted into the early 20th century.

▲ President Paul Kruger visits injured British soldiers in the Transvaal. Ward sanitation improved significantly in the late 19th century.

▶ Florence Nightingale (1820–1910) raised the profile of military healthcare during the Crimean War. She argued vociferously for cleanliness and good food as key tools to assist recovery.

THE LIFE OF THE OFFICER

Although the colonies offered plentiful opportunities for a career officer to feather his nest, they could also be places of hardship and dangerous service for even the most privileged classes, who were by no means immune to disease and violence.

The colonies were alluring postings for ambitious officers, old and young. For many, the journey to a colony was just part and parcel of a regimental deployment, but many officers actually volunteered for overseas service. For example, young German officers often faced the choice between a posting to a rather dull and predictable life of administration in an east German frontier garrison, or a far more exciting life in exotic Africa. Overseas there seemed to be more chances of a pampered existence (often at the expense of the local population), combat, promotion, enhanced reputation, and a better chance to acquire and practice valuable skills, such as military engineering. Others were lured by the prospects of wealth or salacious stories of native women.

▲ Indian princes and British Army officers in the Hyderabad contingent polo team. Polo was an elite sport, requiring personal wealth.

MIXED FATES

The reality of officer life was much more variable, depending on the campaign and country. Some officers would find themselves plunged into hellish campaigns in desolate, flyblown regions, where life was short for all ranks. During German campaigns in Africa in the early 20th century, it was found that in combat officers were nearly twice as likely to be killed as other ranks. The converse was true of the effects of disease, the likeliest explanation being that the higher standards of food and accommodation experienced by officers gave them stronger immune systems to fight off infection and illness.

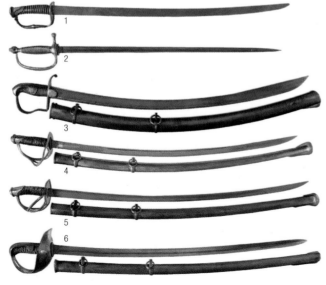

◀ A collection of officers' swords from the 19th century:
1 Officer's saber with hilt modifications;
2 Model 1840 musician's sword with brass hilt;
3 1796 light cavalry saber with iron scabbard;
4 Model 1860 light cavalry saber with iron scabbard;
5 Model 1840 heavy cavalry saber with iron scabbard;
6 19th-century heavy cavalry saber with iron scabbard.

SOCIAL MATTERS

Officers in long-established colonies would frequently live and serve alongside their families. During the 18th and early 19th centuries, it was not uncommon (although it was frowned on) for British officers in India to strike up relationships with indigenous women. With the establishment of the British Raj (when the British government took over administration of India from the East India Company), it became more common for officers to bring their wives with them and establish families. The wives also had to adjust to the social niceties of rank. At social events, for example, women had to leave the room in descending order of their husbands' ranks, leaving the wives of humble lieutenants and captains under no illusions about their station.

The chief leisure pursuit of officers in the colonies was hunting. Tiger hunting was especially popular in India, often conducted from the back of a regally attired elephant. An estimated 380 tigers were shot by the colonists in India every year, resulting in a dramatic decline in the population.

▼ A British officer in India receives a pedicure from an Indian servant. Such status reinforced a misplaced sense of cultural superiority.

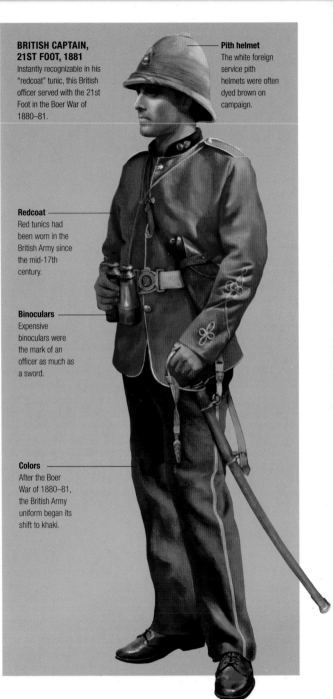

BRITISH CAPTAIN, 21ST FOOT, 1881
Instantly recognizable in his "redcoat" tunic, this British officer served with the 21st Foot in the Boer War of 1880–81.

Pith helmet
The white foreign service pith helmets were often dyed brown on campaign.

Redcoat
Red tunics had been worn in the British Army since the mid-17th century.

Binoculars
Expensive binoculars were the mark of an officer as much as a sword.

Colors
After the Boer War of 1880–81, the British Army uniform began its shift to khaki.

UNIFORMS IN THE 19TH CENTURY

Colonial service in distant lands soon revealed the shortcomings of uniforms that were perfectly serviceable in the more benign climates of European environments.

The British experience in India and Africa in the 19th century illustrates perfectly how colonial service revealed the many deficiencies of uniform design. The classic British redcoat was a dashing item on a parade ground in England, but in the heat and humidity of the tropics it was a terrible burden. The heavy cloth retained sweat, making it hold in heat during the daytime, then turn chilly during the cool evening hours. Stitching rotted, fabric stank, and coats and shirts lasted a fraction of the time they would have done in European climates.

SUPPLY

To keep clothes in good condition, they had to be washed and repaired much more frequently. The result of this was that colonial soldiers tended to be issued more uniform items than soldiers

▼ German soldiers of the late 19th/early 20th century, showing how the lessons of light clothing and helmets had been learned in the tropics.

TROOPER, NATAL CARABINEERS, 1899
The Natal Carabineers were a colonial British force raised in South Africa in 1855. Their uniform was a mix of local and British Army elements.

Cartridges
Cartridges for the Martini-Henry rifle were kept in leather pouches and bandoliers.

Bread bag
The bread bag would have held food supplies.

Legwear
The lower limbs are well protected from the African scrub in leather shoes and calf protectors.

▲ An image of the classic British Redcoats. Every item of clothing would be inappropriate, uncomfortable, and unhygienic in the humid heat of the tropics.

in Europe. A British cavalryman in India described his kit as: "6 pairs of white trowsers [sic], 6 pairs of draws [sic], 3 flannel shirts, 6 shirts, 4 white jackets, 4 puggerees, 6 pairs socks, 1 pair *sefferen* trousers [ribbed wool]; for watering order: 2 pairs blue clothern overalls, 1 blue stable jacket, 1 dress coat, 1 shako, 1 cloak, 2 pairs of boots. Besides these we had many fancy things, not regimental." The practical workload for regimental laundry must have been severe.

ADAPTED CLOTHING

As noted previously, the British eventually replaced their bright clothing with khaki, and many European armies made the same evolution during the later 19th century. Partly this is explained by European encounters with practical native dress. During the Boer Wars, for example, the British saw how the Boers shunned any kind of conventional uniform in favor of practical civilian hunting clothing, usually in shades of the browns that perfectly matched the earth and vegetation of the African landscape, while broad-brimmed hats provided real protection for the face and neck from the equatorial sun.

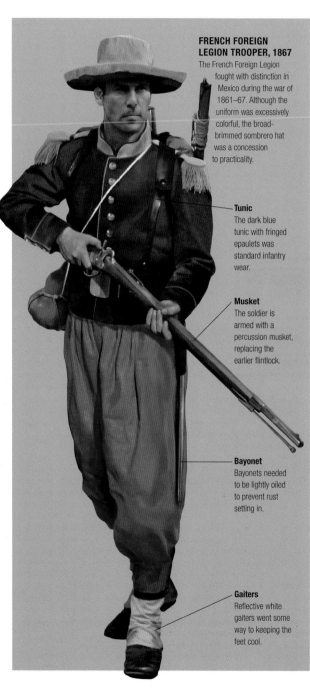

FRENCH FOREIGN LEGION TROOPER, 1867
The French Foreign Legion fought with distinction in Mexico during the war of 1861–67. Although the uniform was excessively colorful, the broad-brimmed sombrero hat was a concession to practicality.

Tunic
The dark blue tunic with fringed epaulets was standard infantry wear.

Musket
The soldier is armed with a percussion musket, replacing the earlier flintlock.

Bayonet
Bayonets needed to be lightly oiled to prevent rust setting in.

Gaiters
Reflective white gaiters went some way to keeping the feet cool.

NATIVE SOLDIERS

Native warriors were inevitably racially patronized by the Europeans and Americans, but their fighting capacities and determination were formidable, as was their ability to live off and move through the land in ways that invading armies found it very difficult to do.

Although indigenous armies generally had little of the organizational complexity of their European enemies, it is incorrect to portray them as uncoordinated and untrained, fighting with only individual aggression.

ZULU REFORMS

The Zulu armies of Africa, for example, were revolutionized by the military and social reforms begun under the monarch Shaka, around 1787–1828. Zulu warriors were organized into a kind of regimental system based on subdivisions by age grouping, with younger warriors serving under the authority of older, more experienced men. Within this system, discipline was brutally enforced—the least sign

▼ Maori chief, Te Hauhau, armed only with traditional wooden weapons, photographed in 1885 in the Waikato, New Zealand, at a time of upheaval and colonization.

▲ The legendary Apache leader Geronimo (far right) with his son and two other braves. Geronimo successfully resisted United States and Mexican expansion into Apache territory for more than 20 years.

of cowardice, physical weakness, or defiance of the leadership could bring a swift and frequently horrible death.

Shaka also changed the weaponry of the individual warrior. Alongside the traditional *assegai* throwing spears and the *knob-kerrie* club, he introduced the shorter *iklwa* stabbing spear, for use in close-quarter combat, with the large *isihlangu* cowhide shield providing protection. Shaka also brought in a form of basic training, ensuring that all his warriors were drilled in core weapons techniques and in how to move en masse in companies or regiments, rather than as a horde of individuals. The Zulus were honed into a formidable army, although the deep traditions of magic and superstition left them vulnerable to the reality of British small arms fire.

TRADITIONS

Many native armies around the world were forced to adapt by their encounters with the foreigners.

MAORI WARFARE

During intertribal Maori conflicts, the warrior tribes would form war parties called *taua*, which could be almost any size. Deception and surprise were much valued in attack, especially during attempts to lure an enemy out from the confines of a fortified village (*pa*). War parties would perform a ritual *haka* dance before coming to blows in violent hand-to-hand combat. After the battle, a ritual cleansing took place.

ZULU WARRIOR, 1879
This Zulu warrior is lightly dressed, but the fur and strips of hide would have given indication of his regiment in the same way as the insignia of a European soldier.

Headdress
The *isicoco* headring was worn by more senior warriors.

Weapons
This warrior is armed with several *assegai* throwing spears.

Shield
The shield is made from oxhide, and could also be used as a shelter at hot times of day.

Leg decoration
Legs might be decorated with hide strips, fur, or animal tails.

> "...as the men fell back **the Zulus came with a rush**, and in a very few minutes it became a hand-to-hand conflict..."
>
> W. DRUMMOND, BRITISH HEADQUARTERS STAFF, REPORT FROM 1879

The Native American warriors, for example, retained much of their traditional weaponry—compound bow, ax, club, dagger—but also enthusiastically embraced firearms, which they found were as useful for hunting as for warfare.

Yet traditionalism remained strong in native ways of war. Among the Plains Indians of North America, there was the practice of "counting coup"—a highly risky business of touching an enemy with a "coup stick" and then making an escape unharmed. Captives were frequently tortured; scalps were removed as a token of the victor's bravery, and prisoners were put through terrible ordeals to judge their mettle.

▼ Japanese samurai warriors in traditional garb. Samurai traditions and weaponry persisted in Japanese culture until the end of World War II.

TACTICAL DEVELOPMENTS

Colonial wars brought the European armies into contact with some new ways of making war. The hardest lessons of all were perhaps learned by the British during the Boer Wars, where they faced what was in effect an expert and determined insurgency.

When the Boers committed themselves to armed resistance against the British in 1880, they appeared to be working at a disadvantage. The British Army was the tip of the spear for the world's greatest empire, and had dominated enemies across the world with courage, discipline, and concentrated firepower. The Boers, by contrast, were essentially a militarized civilian force.

IRREGULAR WARFARE

The Boers formed a true citizen army, with virtually every male between the ages of 16 and 60 eligible for military

▼ British troops in the Boer campaign had to use protected "dead ground" to avoid lethally accurate Boer fire.

▲ A British field position during the Boer War. The earthen bank provides a defensive berm, able to stop even the heaviest-caliber rifle bullet.

"**Almost** before we knew it, we were **swarming**, over the walls, **shooting** and **clubbing** in hand-to-hand conflict. It was **sharp work**."

DENEYS REITZ, A BOER FIGHTER, 1900

service. The Boer force was not a formal army. Rather, it was composed of burghers organized by district, with commandants elected by popular vote.

The Boers were tough fighters, determined, adaptable, and accustomed to hardship through working the land, a land that they knew with careworn intimacy. Hunting and riding were absolute necessities of Boer life, so the Boer fighters were generally excellent shots and horsemen, and could maneuver confidently through the bush. Formed into commando units, the Boers would use stealth to get into rifle range, then hit with lightning speed and from good cover to inflict heavy casualties on the British ranks before fleeing to fight another day. In some unequal engagements, British troops took more than 200 losses while the Boers lost fewer than 10 men.

CHANGING WAYS

The British adapted to the harrowing losses with enough strategic (rather than tactical) innovation to secure victory in the Boer War, but the lesson had been learned. In the colonial conflicts, mobility, good cover, and accurate firepower were critical. Soldiers quickly learned the distinction between cover and concealment. Concealment shielded you from view by the enemy, but it provided no

▲ A Boer commando unit. Note the light hunting clothing and the heavy-caliber hunting rifles, lethal out to 650 yards/600 m and beyond.

▼ British munitions: 1 paper-wrapped dynamite; 2 and 3 cast-iron hand grenades; 4 a shrapnel shell, showing a cutaway of the warhead (image not to scale); 5–8 four types of rifle cartridge, for the Snider (5) Martini-Henry (6 and 7) and Lee-Enfield (8) rifles.

physical protection from bullets (such as a thick bush). Cover, by contrast, gave the soldier visual and physical protection, and therefore had to be sought once the bullets began flying. The colonial wars taught many armies, including those of France, Germany, and America, the principles of fieldcraft and fire-and-maneuver that we now take for granted as the cornerstones of infantry tactics.

◀ The Boers were experts in battlefield movement, although horses were the more typical mode of transport, rather than this ingenious adaptation of two bicycles for rail use.

FACETS OF WAR: CIVILIANS

When countries go to war, the civilian populations almost always suffer as much, if not more, than the actual combatants. Throughout history, the relationship of civilians to military forces has been complex, and frequently tragic.

While military history often focuses on the soldiers doing the fighting, the overall ability of a nation to propagate conflict depends on its civilian population. Most importantly, civilians have to man and maintain essential war industries. During World War II in Britain, for example, 48,000 men were recruited directly into the coal-mining industry from 1943, rather than the armed forces. The "Bevin Boys" (named after Ernest Bevin, the Minister of Labour and National Service) helped ensure that the essential raw material supply was unaffected by the loss of manpower to the military. It was vital, dangerous war work that brought little glamour or recognition.

WOMEN AND CHILDREN

War has a particularly profound effect on women and children. Historically, women and children frequently

▼ Camp followers—families of Union Army soldiers are here seen living at the camp of the 31st Pennsylvania Infantry during the Civil War, 1862.

accompanied husbands or sons to war as "camp followers." Strictly speaking, this category includes any civilians who follow military forces into the field. In this role the women provided the army with essential menial duties, such as laundry, cooking, foraging, and, it has to be acknowledged, sexual services. By performing such tasks, the camp followers boosted morale among the soldiery and also helped maintain the logistical efficiency of the force. In return, they received protection and provisions from the military, so were both burden and assistance to the soldiery. Sometimes the presence of camp followers had tragic results, as enemy forces often didn't look kindly on those who bolstered their opponents. Back in antiquity, the utter destruction of Roman legions in the Teutoburg Forest in 9BC included the

▲ German security forces round up Jews for deportation in Warsaw, Poland. In addition to the murders in the death camps, 1.1 million Jews were executed in the field.

▼ During wartime, the line between civilian and combatant is often blurred. Tens of thousands of Russian civilians, like the two below, joined partisan forces.

▲ During the defense of Leningrad, in World War II, Russian civilians prepare antitank ditches. Untrained civilians also performed roles such as medics and firemen.

▼ Modern armies recognize that they must win the trust of local civilian populations if they are to develop a secure operating environment. Here a U.S. Marine in Afghanistan in 2009 spends some time talking with Afghan children. United States military forces have also built schools within Afghanistan.

killing or enslavement of some 10,000–20,000 civilians. A similar tragedy unfolded in Afghanistan in 1842, during the British retreat from Kabul.

CIVILIANS AS TARGETS

A terrible fact of war is that civilians are often the very object of military action. Sometimes this is on account of retribution or a fostered lust for destruction. The massacre of up to 300,000 Chinese civilians by the Japanese in Nanking in 1937–38 is a dreadful example, although not isolated in history. At other times the focus has been ideological or racial, with no more appalling example than the German-unleashed Holocaust of 1941–45. Yet often the civilians are simply in the way, the victims of strategic bombing (as in World War II), urban fighting, or the passage of enemy forces through their homelands. More enlightened soldiers realize, however, that winning civilian "hearts and minds" can be the key to ultimate victory.

TIMELINE

9BC Some 20,000 camp followers are either killed or enslaved when a large Roman legionary force is destroyed by German tribes in the Teutoburg Forest, Lower Saxony.

1099 Crusader troops massacre tens of thousands of Muslims, Jews, and Eastern Christians following the siege of Jerusalem.

15th century From this century onward, permanent standing armies become more common in Europe and elsewhere, making a clearer social division between soldiers and civilians.

1793 The *levée en masse* in revolutionary France mobilizes the entire population for war. Civilians play an integral part in the war effort, from fundraising to actual fighting.

1842 The British Army suffers one of its greatest disasters when a huge column of soldiers and 12,000 camp followers is destroyed by Afghan tribesmen during the retreat from Kabul.

1918–45 During both World Wars, women become central to the war effort by working in industry, occupying jobs previously held by men away in the armed services.

1941–44 Leningrad in northern Russia is besieged by the Germans for 900 days. The civilian population play their part in an epic defense but at a terrible price—more than 600,000 citizens die of starvation.

1943–45 The German civilian population and its housing is directly targeted by the Allied strategic bombing campaign.

1949 The Geneva Convention is extended to include protection for civilian populations.

THE BOXER REBELLION

This two-year rebellion in China against its occupiers was as much about a clash of culture as about Chinese national politics. The contrast between the European soldiers and the Chinese insurgents was pronounced, in everything from uniform to spiritual outlook.

The Boxer Rebellion began in 1899, and rumbled on with peaks of violence until 1901. It began with violent attacks on European citizens by Chinese nationalists known as "Boxers," but was eventually suppressed by troops of an eight-nation alliance—Britain, Russia, Japan, France, United States, Germany, Italy, and Austria-Hungary.

BOXERS
The Boxers originated in northern China. As their label suggests, they were trained in martial arts, and each village unit of 25–100 men would be led by a "Senior Brother Disciple," an individual known for his superior fighting skills. They dressed in the colorful style of martial artists, with vivid caps, turbans, gowns, sashes, scarves, and leggings. There was also a force of female boxers

▲ German occupation troops leave Tientsin in 1906. Kaiser Wilhelm II said the Chinese should "tremble at the approach of a German."

▼ A Russian military camp in Stretensk. Each infantry squad has stacked its rifles and kit together, keeping gun muzzles clear of dirt.

EYEWITNESS ACCOUNT

"...the rifle-firing and cannonading were fearful, bullets, balls, and shells falling in all directions. In the midst of the general confusion a large company of Chinese [some regular Chinese forces supported the Boxers]—some 200—were discovered creeping along close to the wall toward the American legation. They were fired upon by our troops, and 30 or 40 were killed. If we could realize the situation it would be a fearful thing to feel one's self in the focus of all this murderous hate and devilry."
—Missionary J.H. Ross, describing a Boxer attack on July 13, 1900

PRIVATE, GERMAN EAST ASIAN BRIGADE, 1900
The German East Asian Brigade was a force sent to protect European citizens in Beijing/Peking in 1900. This individual is wearing the field-gray winter uniform introduced in 1901.

Rifle
The bolt-action rifle is the new 7.92-mm Gewehr 98.

Ammo pouches
The leather pouches held five-round clips of 7.92-mm ammunition.

Breeches
The riding breeches and cavalry boots indicate this man belongs to a mounted unit.

known as the Red Lanterns, based around Tientsien.

Spirituality was important to the Boxer warrior. Each recruit underwent a magical initiation ritual that was meant to make him or her invulnerable to bullets (a belief soon debunked).

OVERSEAS TROOPS

The foreign armies sent to China were conventional European-style troops. As well as modern rifles and artillery—as opposed to the traditional edged weapons usually carried by the Boxers—the allied forces brought with them very different cultural outlooks. Most European and American soldiers were of Protestant, Catholic, Orthodox, or, less commonly, Jewish religious backgrounds, their religious upbringing often infused with an imperial sense of the divine right to rule over others.

Religious differences were critical to the commitment brought to the conflict by each side. The Boxer soldiers, holding Western Christian influence as heavily to blame for China's problems, massacred Christian European communities and Chinese converts. Conversely, the allied troops viewed the Boxer faith as dangerous spiritualism, and delivered a punishing victory.

▼ Russian marines use concentrated fire from their rifles to repel a major Boxer attack in the embassy district of Beijing in 1900.

HORSE AND SOLDIER

The horse has a long history of participation in war, despite the fact that in many ways its character is unsuited to battle. The soldier's relationship with the horse during the colonial era depended, as always, on the personality of the soldier and the nature of the campaign.

The horse was central to imperialism. Without mounted personnel providing the principal means of in-country logistics, nations such as Britain, France, Italy, and Germany would have been unable to consolidate and administer vast swathes of territory. Yet despite its absolute importance, the life of the military horse was generally not a happy one.

ANIMAL INVESTMENT

Although some horses would be shipped out with a colonial army, most of them would be purchased from local suppliers. In fact, this made sense, as European horses were not acclimatized to tropical conditions—many of these unfortunate creatures died within weeks of arrival, killed by heat, overwork, and disease. But the sourcing of local animals could be a headache for a unit's logisticians or for cavalry forces.

▲ British artillery troopers attempt to maneuver along a narrow road through the Khyber Pass in Afghanistan.

▼ A column of horses advance toward Johannesburg in 1901. Horses were as prone to heat exhaustion as the men.

Aware that supply might outstrip demand, local traders could sell weak or old horses at grossly inflated prices, only for the soldiers to see the animals drop dead within days. The soldier's job, therefore, was to keep the animal alive and well for as long as possible.

CARE AND UPKEEP

A soldier whose job it was to look after a horse had to meet the animal's substantial requirements for food and water if it were to perform at its best. On campaign, each horse could require a daily ration of up to 18 pounds/8 kg of hay and 8 pounds/4 kg of corn.

● ●

> "The bullets came among us like hailstones ...The horses came off worse."
>
> GUNNER ALBERT H. BUTLER, DESCRIBING THE BATTLE OF COLENSO, BOER WAR, 1899

● ●

▲ A dismounted lancer during a skirmishing display in 1896 shows a method for turning his horse into a defensive barricade, plus a firing platform on which he can steady his aim and fire.

Furthermore, even in temperate climates in cool weather, a horse would need about 5 gallons/23 liters of water, so tactical movements had to be planned around places at which horses could be refreshed. Add the requirements to keep the horse well-groomed (essential for limiting exposure to insect-borne diseases) and treated for injury, while maintaining all the many items of horse tack, looking after horses was a responsible and physically demanding job.

Soldiers often became rather callous toward horses, hardened by witnessing so many creatures dying through natural attrition or observing them being killed in huge numbers in battle. Yet there is also evidence that many soldiers became highly attached to their mounts. For example, following the terrible Battle of Omdurman in 1898, soldiers of the 21st Lancers led their mortally wounded horses to running water for one last drink before being compelled to shoot them.

Lance
The lance was effective in open battle, but less useful at close quarters.

TROOPER, 21ST LANCERS, OMDURMAN, 1898
The Battle of Omdurman in the Sudan in 1898 saw some legendary bravery by the 21st Lancers. As their name suggested, Lancers fought from horseback with a lance, and preferred horses more than 15 hands high.

Bandolier
The chest bandolier contains cartridges for a carbine.

Equipage
The horse's equipage is light and basic; in hot climates anything extraneous was removed.

Stirrups
The lancer would push forward in the stirrups to ride out the impact of the lance on a human.

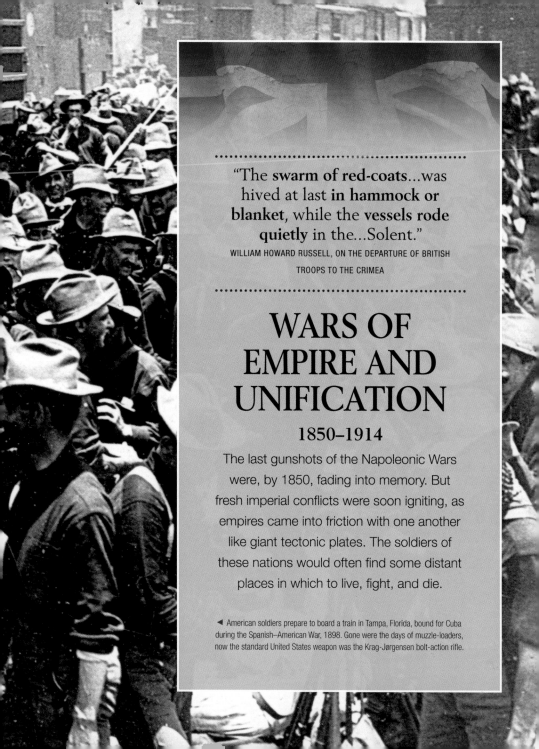

> "The **swarm of red-coats**…was hived at last **in hammock or blanket**, while the **vessels rode quietly** in the…Solent."

WILLIAM HOWARD RUSSELL, ON THE DEPARTURE OF BRITISH TROOPS TO THE CRIMEA

WARS OF EMPIRE AND UNIFICATION

1850–1914

The last gunshots of the Napoleonic Wars were, by 1850, fading into memory. But fresh imperial conflicts were soon igniting, as empires came into friction with one another like giant tectonic plates. The soldiers of these nations would often find some distant places in which to live, fight, and die.

◀ American soldiers prepare to board a train in Tampa, Florida, bound for Cuba during the Spanish–American War, 1898. Gone were the days of muzzle-loaders, now the standard United States weapon was the Krag-Jørgensen bolt-action rifle.

IMPERIAL EXPANSIONS

The 19th century was a period of aggressive imperialism and emerging statehood. New nations were born through unification and independence—such as Germany and Italy—while around the world empires came to blows as they expanded their territories.

The end of the Napoleonic Wars in 1815 by no means meant that all Europe's armies found themselves with time on their hands. The 19th century was a period of intense imperial rivalry, particularly over territories in Africa and Asia, and soon even old allies were brought into conflict.

EMPIRES AND NATIONS

The preeminent imperial power of the 19th century was undoubtedly Britain, but its power was by no means uncontested on the world stage. Russia in particular was a major strategic rival, whose expansion into Central Asia made the British government feel that its colonial hold over India, and influence over neighboring Afghanistan,

▲ U.S. Army signal corps soldiers during the Spanish–American War use a heliograph to send signals to other units.

▼ General Frederick Funston (right) takes a meal with two other officers in the field in Cuba, 1898. He was eventually forced from the campaign by an acute bout of malaria.

were threatened. The tensions bubbled up into some major conflicts, especially the Crimean War of 1853–56, in which a British, French, Ottoman, and Sardinian alliance inflicted a seminal defeat on the Russian Army, although at heavy cost to all the forces involved. Yet the "Great Game" (as the rivalry between Russia and Britain was

PROPAGANDA

Propaganda has long been a tool of governments, used to shape the beliefs of their soldiers and citizens. During the 19th century, the primary tools of propaganda were print media (newspapers, leaflets, cartoons and so on) but also messages dispersed through official, respected bodies, such as state-sanctioned religions or direct from a monarchy.

known) was just one of many imperial conflicts that rippled across the world in the 19th and early 20th centuries. These included the Franco–Mexican War (1861–67), Franco–Prussian War (1870–71), Russo–Turkish War (1877–78), Spanish–American War (1898) and the Russo–Japanese War (1904–05). The imperial clashes also produced struggles for independence and unification in Italy and Germany, spawning unified nations.

▲ Prussian artillery on the Place de la Concorde in Paris, March 1, 1871. The soldiers of the Prussian artillery were known for their efficiency and high rates of fire.

▼ Japanese troops await an attack during the Russo–Japanese War (1904–05). Diaries from Japanese soldiers show they mainly fought for survival, not politics.

FIRE AND MANEUVER

The soldiers who fought in these conflicts faced age-old challenges of martial bureaucracy and ineffency. In the Crimean War, for example, logistical failures resulted in terrible deprivation for the frontline troops. The Russian forces experienced similar struggles during the Russo–Japanese War, waiting weeks for essential supplies and suffering under command incompetence.

But the second half of the 19th century became increasingly unforgiving of such poor leadership. The breech-loading revolution, in both small arms and artillery, had fully established itself by the 1870s. In part this meant that the individual soldier was personally better armed or supported, but it also meant that the battlefield was even more detrimental to survival. Officers also had to adjust to the new era of logistics and communications offered by the telegraph and the railroad. By the end of the century it was becoming clear that a good officer required a much better grasp of technology than an officer had done 100 years previously. The world of war was changing.

SOLDIERS AND REVOLUTIONARIES

From the early 1830s, the Italian independence movement began to gather momentum against its imperial Austrian overlords. In the 1860s the Austrian forces found themselves fighting a army of Italian irregulars, passionately committed to self-rule and national unification.

It is important to remember that until 1871, Italy was not a single nation, but rather a collection of independent states mostly governed under the umbrella authority of the Austro-Hungarian Empire.

The Italians fought three major independence wars, in 1848–49, 1859, and finally 1866. France played an inconstant part in these conflicts, at first fighting for Italian independence then cooling toward this ambition. In the end, although the Italians were ultimately defeated in each conflict by the Austro-Hungarian forces, an Italian alliance with Prussia eventually led to an Austrian defeat and a united Italy.

▲ Giuseppe Garibaldi, the Italian freedom fighter. Garibaldi was a pioneer of guerrilla warfare, on both military and political levels.

IMPERIAL DIVERSITY

Whereas many national armies went into something of a decline following the Napoleonic Wars, Austria's imperial commitments kept its soldiery modern. A key problem faced by senior commanders, however, was that the Austro-Hungarian forces were a mixed bag in terms of ethnic and linguistic diversity, with only 28 percent of German-Austrian origin, 18 percent Hungarian, and 44 percent Slavic. Army units could speak any of nine different languages.

To enable cross-unit communication, all soldiers were required to learn 80 standard German command terms,

◀ A scene from the Battle of Volturno (1860). The battle was a victory for the Redshirts, but the costs of the success weakened the revolutionaries.

GARIBALDI

Giuseppe Garibaldi (1807–82) was born in French-controlled Nice, and grew up to become a certified sea captain before becoming involved in Italy's independence movement. He was forced to flee Italy in 1834, and made his way to Brazil and Uruguay, becoming a revolutionary in South America before returning to campaign in Italy. He remains today an icon of Italian nationhood.

▲ French forces make the arduous march through the Moncenisio Pass in the Piedmontese Alps, 1859.

although the informal development of an "Army Slav" dialect in the ranks also assisted understanding.

ITALIAN DEFIANCE

The soldiers of preunification Italy had a primary allegiance to state and regiment. Some of the regiments were high status, such as the Bersaglieri corps of sharpshooters established in 1836, and, postindependence, the Alpini mountain troops, trained to fight and survive in Italy's mountainous north.

The most famous of the Italian rebels against Austro-Hungarian rule were the "Redshirts" led by Giuseppe Garibaldi. Being a guerrilla force, the Redshirts had little in the way of standardization of uniform or kit. Soldiers often went into action with outdated muskets and civilian clothing; the red woollen shirt and gray pants were the only items that gave some appearance of martial uniformity. The Redshirts were a classic guerrilla force in terms of resources and tactics—high on motivation and commitment, low on strategy and logistics. They won some victories but were eventually crushed by the more northerly forces.

TUSCAN JÄGER, 1848
This soldier wears an Austrian-type Jäger uniform, which consisted of a blue-gray coat and pants with grass-green collars, cuffs, and piping. The hat is Corsican in style.

Blanket
Large woollen blankets could be formed into improvised shelters.

Cross belt
The cross belt includes a percussion cap pouch in the center.

Bayonet
Fitting the bayonet affected the gun's center of gravity.

BREECH-LOADING WEAPONS

The progressive switch from muzzle-loading to breech-loading weapons had a profound effect on the individual soldier. It not only affected how he fought and how he behaved tactically, it also changed the nature of his kit and uniform.

Breech-loading weapons have a venerable ancestry, with some specimens dating back to the 17th century. Yet as standard-issue military weapons, it was only in the second half of the 19th century that they became pervasive and then essential, so that muzzle-loaders were virtually gone from battlefields by the 1880s.

ADVANTAGES

Breech-loading small arms are weapons loaded with unitary cartridges (ammunition that combines the case, gunpowder, primer, and bullet in one unit) from the breech end of the gun

▼ The Gatling Gun was a hand-cranked multibarrel machine gun, developed by American Richard Gatling in 1861. In action, it could fire up to 400 rounds per minute.

▲ The Dreyse Needle Gun was used by the Prussians with great effect during the Austro–Prussian War, here at the Battle of Königgratz on July 3, 1866.

rather than the muzzle. In the 19th century, they offered several key advantages to the soldier—faster reloading and shooting times (especially from a bolt-action magazine feed); greater power, range, and accuracy; improved resilience to damp or wet weather conditions; and improvements in weapon reliability.

These advantages had a profound effect in reshaping the individual soldier's relationship with his weapon. First, he became more lethal than ever—with a modern breech-loading rifle, he could lay down fire out to beyond 660 yards/600 m at rates of up to 15rpm, with a realistic

Breech-loading and percussion weapons of the 19th century: 1 .577 Martini-Henry; 2 15.4-mm Dreyse needle gun; 3 7.63-mm Mauser C/96; 4 .455 Adams 1854 revolver; 5 .44 Winchester 1873; 6 11-mm Mauser 1871.

. . . .

"...if I could invent a machine [gun] ...it would, to a great extent, supersede the necessity of large armies."

RICHARD GATLING

. . . .

expectation of hitting a human-size target. This had a knock-on effect—units no longer needed to rely on volley fire to be influential. It also meant that all men needed marksmanship training; the weapon was now only as accurate as the person wielding it.

The soldier's firearm also became more trustworthy. The days of a firearm going off with a fizzle rather than a bang largely disappeared. Once metallic cartridges were introduced, the propellant was well protected inside its watertight metal housing, meaning that even in the wettest weather conditions a soldier would still be able to continue firing. This being said, the soldier still had to take natural precautions against ammunition getting wet, as rust could build up on the outside of the cartridge and this could result in the cartridge misfeeding into the chamber. Daily maintenance of ammunition and weapons was essential.

EFFECTS ON KIT

The effect of the adoption of breech-loading firearms wasn't merely confined to the soldier's ability to deliver firepower. It also had an effect on kit and uniform. Regarding the former, soldiers now required redesigned ammunition pouches that conveniently held either single rounds or clips of cartridges that fed into the rifle's magazine as a block. In many ways, breech-loading metallic ammunition simplified the soldier's kit, because he no longer needed separate pouches or containers for powder, ball, percussion cap, flint, and all the other various accoutrements that were required for musketry. Ultimately, the power, range, and accuracy of breech-loading weapons also meant that the defiantly colorful uniforms of the past had to go. Anything that increased a soldier's visibility was a bad thing in the breech-loading age.

THE CRIMEAN WAR

Fought between 1853 and 1856, the Crimean War is known for its calamities and heroism, from the terrible effects of disease through to the tragic charge of the Light Brigade at Balaklava. Yet despite its strategic and tactical failures, the conflict also brought important innovations.

The Crimean War brought old European allies and enemies together in the largest conflict since the Napoleonic Wars, albeit in new combinations. This time the British, French, and Ottoman Turks were allied against Russia, opposing Russian imperial expansion around the Black Sea.

EXPOSURE

The conflict is regarded by many as the one in which modern war reporting was born, especially (for the British) with the reports of William Howard Russell. What Russell helped expose, in excruciating detail, was not only the experience of some of the great battles of the war, but also the consequences of chronic failures in British logistics.

British mismangement of logistics in the Crimea is now legendary. Failures included not supplying the transport to

◄ Typical personal items of a British infantryman in the Crimea: 1 backpack; 2 water canteen; 3 sewing kit; 4 playing cards; 5 matches; 6 candle tin; 7 toothbrush; 8–9 mess tins; 10 biscuit; 11 cutlery; 12 tobacco tin; 13 Bible.

◄ A scene from the Battle of Inkerman shows the British 3rd Battalion Grenadier Guards in action. Fought on November 5, 1854, the battle was waged in thick fog.

▲ On the left is the Crimean medal, a campaign medal issued to all British troops, and on the right is the Turkish equivalent.

EYEWITNESS ACCOUNT

"The work for the English troops here is dreadfully hard, and is killing the men; what is most trying is what are called covering parties—large bodies of men are marched down every night to the entrenchments and remain there 24 hours, to prevent the Russians from entering the batteries... Whatever the weather may be there the men have to stay, and, as their clothing is very insufficient, the men are sometimes half dead with cold. Nothing like a fire can be lit, as it would immediately bring upon us...fire."
—Captain Collin Campbell, 1854

take supplies from harbor to troops; not supplying building materials (essential for making huts, as winter approached in 1854); sending limited food, or food that perished too quickly. To compound the problem, a huge storm in Balaklava Harbor on November 14, 1854, destroyed 30 ships and £3,000,000 worth of stores.

The consequences of these issues were horrendous for the British troops that Crimean winter. Men were forced to survive the harsh weather in unheated, thin tents or mud-sodden trenches. Hundreds succumbed to disease or exposure. Food was scarce and of poor quality, and uniform items might go unchanged for weeks. The plight of wounded soldiers was particularly dreadful, often left without treatment for days on bare earth floors, and was much publicized by the work of Florence Nightingale.

INNOVATION

If there was an upside to the horrors of Crimean War conditions, it lay in the responsive procedural and technical innovations that would improve

▲ The British 4th Light Dragoons encamped in the Crimea, 1855. The tents proved inadequate for winter conditions.

▼ Soldiers of the 8th Hussars prepare a meal. Official daily rations for the British included 17 ounces/ 480 g fresh meat, 14 ounces/450 g bread and 2 ounces/50 g sugar.

soldiers' lives in the decades to come. Nightingale, for example, implemented hygiene policies that dramatically reduced deaths from infection. The Russians improved amputation techniques. Chef Alexis Soyer gave the British the "Soyer Stove," a type of fuel-efficient, all-weather portable stove still in British service 120 years later.

THE FRANCO–PRUSSIAN WAR

The victory of the German states over France in the war of 1870–71 not only consolidated the position of Prussia as an expanding European empire, it also proved the quality of its soldiery.

A key difference between the German and French armies during the Franco–Prussian War (1870–71) was that the German states formed their armies primarily from conscription, whereas the French had a mainly volunteer army, supplemented by a large but rather disorganized body of reservists.

GERMAN CONSCRIPTS

The Prussian conscript was typically called up into the forces at the age of 20. After two to three years of service (the length varied slightly according to the branch of army), the man then went through several stages of reserve service, up to the age of 45.

In the decades immediately before the Franco–Prussian War, the German forces had undergone an intense period of modernization, and as such the German soldiers (especially those of Prussia) were generally well-drilled and properly led. This professionalism was

▼ Prussian Uhlans seizing a farm in Lorraine, France. Farms have always been inevitable targets for hungry and scavenging troops.

BAVARIAN TROOPER, 1870
This Bavarian soldier is a member of the 3rd Chevaulegers Regiment, a light horse unit that served in the Franco–Prussian War.

Facings
Pink facings were worn by the 3rd and 6th Regiments.

Saber
The light cavalry used a curved saber for close-quarter fighting.

Color
The chevaulegers had a green tunic, pants, and hair helmet plume.

Boots
This man is wearing over-the-knee heavy cavalry boots.

> ## "The French took off their hats...pointed to their stomachs, and made **gestures indicative of hunger.**"
> GERMAN OFFICER AT METZ, 1870

aided by the fact that many veterans from previous conflicts were in the ranks. The German infantry was also well armed, with the bolt-action Dreyse needle gun. The Prussian military leadership had also invested in a system of basic rations. In previous conflicts, staples of bread and soup had proved difficult to store and transport. So in 1867 Heinrich Grüneberg, at the army's behest, invented the *Erbswurst* sausage. Made of dried bacon and pea flour, it could be stored for long periods and rehydrated to eat on campaign.

FRENCH SOLDIERS
The mobilization of the French soldiers for the Franco–Prussian War left a lot to be desired in terms of organization. Unlike the efficient localized system of Prussian call-up, the French reservists often had to travel long distances before they reached their units. Moreover, discipline was often poor among both regular and reservist forces, an effect of inadequate order in the barracks together with deficient leadership.

Problems with discipline were compounded by a heavy intake of alcohol among the French ranks. French consumption of alcohol appears to have reached new heights at this time, with wine drunk throughout the day followed by a powerful brandy nicknamed the "gut-wringer" at night. At least the French soldier was well armed, the Chassepot rifle being superior to the Prussian Dreyse.

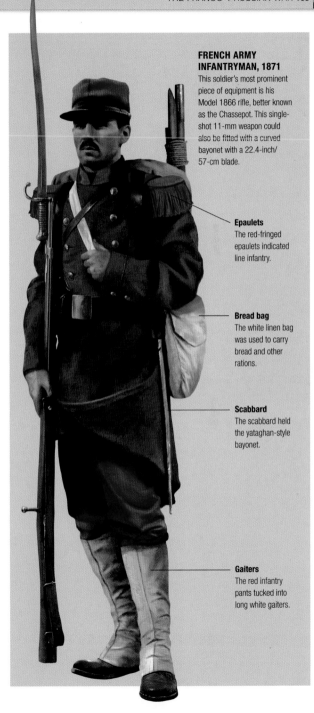

FRENCH ARMY INFANTRYMAN, 1871
This soldier's most prominent piece of equipment is his Model 1866 rifle, better known as the Chassepot. This single-shot 11-mm weapon could also be fitted with a curved bayonet with a 22.4-inch/57-cm blade.

Epaulets
The red-fringed epaulets indicated line infantry.

Bread bag
The white linen bag was used to carry bread and other rations.

Scabbard
The scabbard held the yataghan-style bayonet.

Gaiters
The red infantry pants tucked into long white gaiters.

RUSSIANS AND OTTOMANS

The Russian and Ottoman armies fought each other in four major conflicts during the 19th century, as their respective empires jockeyed for position in Southern and Eastern Europe, with troops of highly variable quality.

The great challenge the Russian Army has always faced is how to balance the demands of size and quality. During the 19th century, Russia could field vast armies (by 1900 it was capable of mobilizing about 4 million men), but feeding, housing, and training such monstrous, often widely spread, levels of manpower remained problematic.

RECRUITMENT

Prior to 1874, the common ranks of the Russian Army were drawn from the country's vast population of rural serfs and its urban poor. Annually, each commune was obliged to put forward the names of a certain percentage of men who were eligible for military service. For obvious reasons, the commune got rid of antisocial or

▶ Russian troops cross the Danube into Bulgaria. A key challenge of amphibious actions was keeping gunpowder dry.

- -

"**The Turkish foot soldier**... is capable of enduring great privation, and a good marcher."

MAJOR F. MAURICE, 1877

- -

▼ Battle of Shipka Pass, 1877. Here Bulgarian volunteers, fighting on the side of the Russians, use rocks to fight off attacks by Turkish forces.

unproductive individuals by putting them at the top of their list, which didn't do the quality of the Russian Army any favors. Interestingly, once men had entered service, they technically became freemen, no longer obligated to their former service to the state or a landowner. Hard and spartan conditions in the army, however, more than offset any sense of privilege.

The recruitment system was open to exploitation and was also blatantly unfair, with about 20 percent of the male population protected from such rough service by virtue of high birth or education. On January 1, 1874, however, universal conscription by ballot was placed on all males between the ages of 21 and 43.

On the Ottoman side, prior to reforms between 1837 and 1848, recruitment was performed on a similar basis to that of pre-1874 Russia. However, the reforms introduced more regular and equitable conscription. The Ottomans sought to modernize their army in many other ways, particularly in terms of weaponry and kit, hence

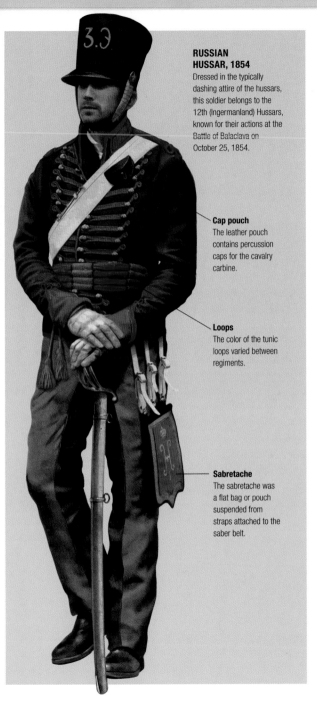

RUSSIAN HUSSAR, 1854
Dressed in the typically dashing attire of the hussars, this soldier belongs to the 12th (Ingermanland) Hussars, known for their actions at the Battle of Balaclava on October 25, 1854.

Cap pouch
The leather pouch contains percussion caps for the cavalry carbine.

Loops
The color of the tunic loops varied between regiments.

Sabretache
The sabretache was a flat bag or pouch suspended from straps attached to the saber belt.

many men were armed with the latest Martini-Peabody and Snider rifles.

CAMPAIGN CONDITIONS
The conditions on campaign in both Russian and Ottoman forces were generally grim. For a start, both armies continued to suffer extremely high rates of attrition from disease, especially in the first half of the century. Even during peacetime, losses from illness were in the region of 10 percent.

The Russo–Turkish Wars in the Caucasus were hard affairs for both sides, fought in unforgiving terrain, often at long distances from logistical hubs. This meant inevitable shortages at the frontlines. It has been estimated that in the Russian Army, for example, up to 90 percent of the total food supplies in a resupply column might be eaten by the time it reached its intended destination, on account of the length of the journey undertaken.

▼ Russian peasant veteran soldiers from the Russo–Turkish Wars; finding employment after many decades in military service could be a challenge.

NEW AMERICAN WARS

The Spanish–American War (1898) and the Philippine–American War (1899–1902) forced the United States armed forces to take a long, hard look at the way they mobilized, deployed, and fought. Difficult lessons were learned, but they helped the U.S. Army professionalize.

Although the Civil War ended in 1865, the sheer scale of that conflict's devisiveness cast a long shadow over the rest of the century.

REGULARS AND MILITIA

After the Civil War, the American land army reverted to a mix of regular and state militia troops. The regular forces fell in numbers precipitously—by 1890 they numbered only 27,300 men. Many of these soldiers found themselves in rather dull duties manning frontier forts or coastal defenses, but others gained combat experience through the numerous conflicts with Native Americans that rumbled on into the late 19th century. Still, the fact remained that the U.S. Army was not an organization capable of fighting a major national or international conflict.

▲ Men of the Rough Riders pose for a photograph. At first, many new recruits brought their own weapons and equipment.

▼ Typical U.S. infantry kit of the Spanish–American War: 1 backpack and drinking cup; 2 cartridge belt and bayonet; 3 pistol belt; 4 haversack; 5 water canteen.

In addition to the regular army, however, there was a large state militia of around 100,000 men, which increasingly began to adopt the now-familiar title of National Guard. The National Guard soldier was essentially a militarized, unpaid civilian. He was trained in basic drill about once a week, with a weeklong camp once a year.

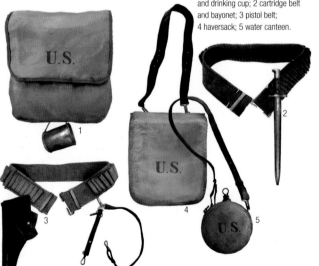

EYEWITNESS ACCOUNT

"Major Eskridge is wounded severely but not dangerously. Maj. Lincoln had his thigh broken and in falling either broke or badly sprained his arm—Captain Duggan is wounded, according to the papers... Koop got a rap in the head from the same bullet that hit me, the Spanish killing two birds with one stone, but Carl's head always was hard and it did not do a thing to the bullet but flatten it."
—Letter from Lt. Eli Helmick to his wife, Spanish–American War, 1898

U.S. ARMY SOLDIER, CUBA, 1898

Apart from the wide-brimmed campaign hat, the uniform of the American soldier in 1898 was similar to that worn by U.S. troops during the Civil War.

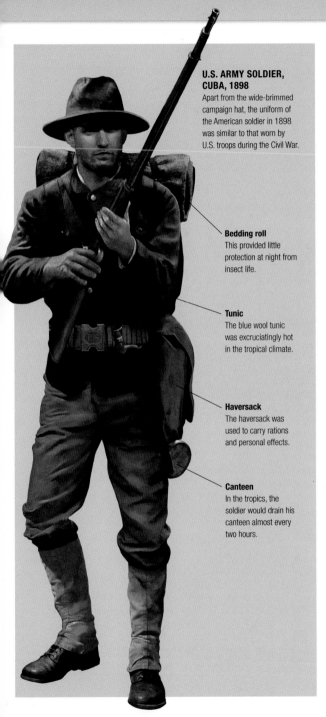

Bedding roll
This provided little protection at night from insect life.

Tunic
The blue wool tunic was excruciatingly hot in the tropical climate.

Haversack
The haversack was used to carry rations and personal effects.

Canteen
In the tropics, the soldier would drain his canteen almost every two hours.

▲ U.S. soldiers bound for Cuba wait at the dockside. Note the distinctive "Montana Peak" campaign hat to the left, which was good at handling tropical downpours.

ROUGH RIDERS

The outbreak of the Spanish–American War in 1898 forced the United States government into a massive recruitment drive for overseas service in Cuba and the Philippines. Volunteers from the National Guard formed the bulk of the recruits, but there were also three regular volunteer cavalry regiments. The most famous of these was the 1st United States Volunteer Cavalry, better known as the "Rough Riders," led by a young Theodore Roosevelt.

The Rough Riders were recruited from tough men used to riding and surviving in the arid south and southwest of the United States. In action, the men could handle rifles and pistols effectively, both from horseback and when dismounted. To set the Rough Riders apart from the rest of the army, they developed a certain flamboyant appearance, with a slouch hat, cavalry breeches, and a colored kerchief knotted around the neck; the latter proving useful for the sweat-inducing tropical conditions found in Cuba and the Philippines.

FACETS OF WAR: WAR REPORTING

Professional war reporting is a relatively recent phenomenon in military history. Yet it has had a dramatic effect on the way that conflicts are viewed and even fought, so inevitably censorship has generally followed hand in hand with reportage.

Firsthand journalistic reporting from a war zone began in earnest during the 19th century, although we can find precedents. In some senses, ancient works such as Thucydides' *History of the Peloponnesian War* (5th century BC) and Xenophon's *Anabasis* (4th century BC) are early examples, providing factual accounts of military campaigns and operations. Similar examples are found in the medieval period, but it was the birth of newspapers in the 17th century that really began the demand for frontline reporting.

BRINGING THE NEWS HOME

History's first war correspondent was arguably John Bell, who reported on the Duke of York's campaigns in the Netherlands in 1794 for the London-based *Oracle and Public Advertiser*.

▲ Born in Bennington, Kansas, Peggy Hull was the United States' first female war correspondent, covering both World Wars.

▼ Marcus Sparling, assistant to history's first war photographer, Roger Fenton, sits on the front of their specialized photographic wagon in the Crimea, 1855.

TIMELINE

5th century BC The Greek historian Thucydides writes his *History of the Peloponnesian War*.

1415 French knight Jean de Waurin provides firsthand accounts of the Battle of Agincourt.

1794 John Bell reports on an artillery cannonade in Belgium for the *Oracle and Public Advertiser*.

1807 The London *Times* hires Henry Crabb Robinson to report on the Napoleonic Wars.

1854–56 The brutally honest reporting on the Crimean War by William Howard Russell has a major effect on British public opinion.

1861–65 During the American Civil War, more than 1,500 newspapers take stories from frontline correspondents.

1914–18 Most combatants establish systems by which officially approved reporters are embedded with frontline forces.

1939–45 War reporting becomes an established part of factual journalism but also propaganda, such as through the German magazine *Signal*.

1963–75 Reporting on the Vietnam War is presented through print, photojournalism, and TV, fueling antiwar public opinion.

1976–Present Satellite and then internet systems transform the speed of news from the field.

VISUAL REPORTING

War reporting in the 20th century was transformed by visual media, first photography and then moving pictures for cinema and TV. In World War II, some 10,000 journalists of all nationalities took their place on the frontline, and people such as Ernie Pyle, Chester Wilmot, and Ilya Ehrenburg became household names.

It was during the subsequent Vietnam War that war reporting reached new levels of intimacy, showing the horrors of war in unprecedented detail. Such was the adverse effect the reporting had on public opinion, that since then most press reporting from war zones has been tightly controlled by the military authorities. Access to battlefronts, information, and key personnel are policed by diligent press officers. It is via public videos on the internet, therefore, that the most unrestricted war footage is now found.

Other worthy candidates for the title are 19th-century British reporters Henry Crabb Robinson, Charles Lewis Guneison, and William Howard Russell. These pioneers firmly established the tradition of frontline reporting that exists to this day in print and numerous other media.

▲ Hugely popular war reporter Ernie Pyle rests on the roadside with a Marine patrol, Okinawa, April 1945.

▼ An NBC cameraman rides along with U.S. forces in Iraq. Most news teams now have to be approved and authorized by military forces to get good access.

SOLDIERS OF CHINA AND JAPAN

Comparing the soldiers of China and Japan reveals how some Asian armies embraced modernization wholeheartedly, while others clung to traditional ways, and inevitably spiraled into decline, inefficiency, and low morale.

Although much military innovation had taken place in East Asia during the medieval period, by the mid-19th century it was the West that led the world in the new technologies and tactics of soldiering. How the Asian armies responded to that fact could determine, to a large extent, the life of the soldier within those forces.

THE CHINESE ARMY

By the mid-19th century, China undoubtedly had a potent army on paper. If we include its militarized police elements, it had a force of between 500,000 and 800,000 men, many of them tested in China's frequent internal wars and insurrections.

Chinese soldiers were known either as "Bannermen"—soldiers who served under one of eight prestigious banners, defined largely by ethnic origins—or the Green Standard Army, less prestigious

▲ The uniforms and weaponry of these Chinese soldiers from 1885 show how outdated China's army was compared to the Japanese.

▼ Japanese troops land at Chinnampo, March 1904. The Japanese soldiers developed an expertise in amphibious warfare.

(but eventually more numerous) and more ethnically diverse troops. The skills and effectiveness across this spectrum varied considerably. Chinese soldiers dressed traditionally, and some were known for their almost acrobatic ability to fight from horseback.

However, because of the anti-Western undercurrents within much of Chinese society at this time, the Chinese soldier tended to be outdated in terms of his kit and weaponry. In the matter of personal weapons, for example, while the rest of the world shifted to breech-loading cartridge rifles, Chinese soldiers still went into action with spears, bow and arrow, crossbows, and swords. Firearms tended to be muzzle-loading matchlocks or *jingals*, awkward muzzle-loaders that were so large they needed to be

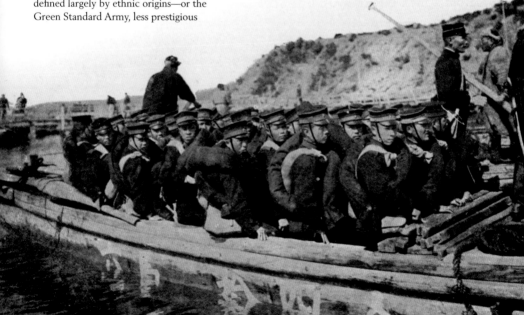

▲ Japanese soldiers were physically hardy men, able to bear heavy loads—such as these ammunition crates—many miles over rough terrain.

propped on a solid object before firing. Many other anachronisms persisted, and they go a long way to explaining the generally poor performance of Chinese soldiers.

THE JAPANESE ARMY

Japanese forces, by contrast, were thoroughly modernized during the 19th century, particularly following the Meiji Restoration of 1868 and the contemporaneous foundation of the Imperial Japanese Army (IJA), which opened the country more to Western influences and improved organization.

The Japanese soldier thus benefited from an advancing professionalization. Standards of training were high, and the kit was basic but of decent standard, including modern bolt-action rifles. From 1869 to 1880, the Japanese soldier was armed with a mix of foreign weapons, including the British Snider-Enfield and the French Chassepot, but in 1880 it produced its first indigenous weapon, the 11-mm Murata Type 13. Variants of the Murata armed the soldiers until 1897, when the army adopted a more modern Arisaka type.

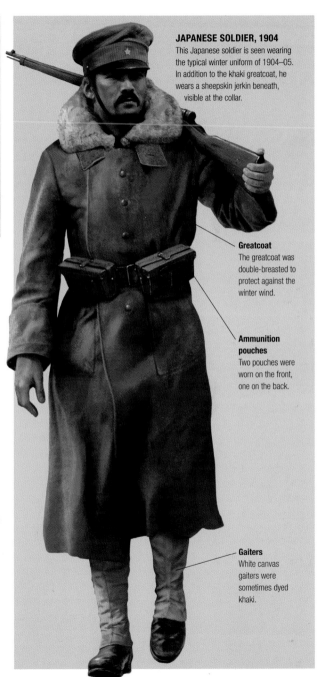

JAPANESE SOLDIER, 1904

This Japanese soldier is seen wearing the typical winter uniform of 1904–05. In addition to the khaki greatcoat, he wears a sheepskin jerkin beneath, visible at the collar.

Greatcoat
The greatcoat was double-breasted to protect against the winter wind.

Ammunition pouches
Two pouches were worn on the front, one on the back.

Gaiters
White canvas gaiters were sometimes dyed khaki.

THE WORLD WARS AND MODERN CONFLICT

WAR, FIGHTING, AND THE ART OF SOLDIERING CHANGED UTTERLY DURING THE 20TH CENTURY. THE MAIN DRIVING FORCE BEHIND THE TRANSFORMATION WAS TECHNOLOGY, WHICH REVOLUTIONIZED EVERYTHING FROM COMMUNICATIONS AND LOGISTICS THROUGH TO UNIFORMS AND WEAPONRY. YET SOME ASPECTS OF THE SOLDIER'S EXPERIENCE REMAINED STUBBORNLY TIMELESS.

◄ U.S. soldiers unload supplies from Coast Guard-manned landing craft along Futatsune Beach, Iwo Jima, after Marines made the initial landings to oppose the Japanese forces occupying the island.

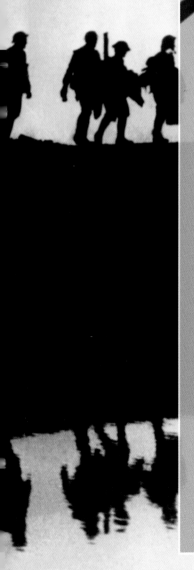

> "The **communication trench** was
> ...about **seven feet deep**, so that
> one's vision was limited to a **patch
> of darkening sky** and the shoulders
> of the man in front."
>
> GUY CHAPMAN, BRITISH ROYAL FUSILIERS

WORLD WAR I

1914–18

World War I was, arguably, history's first global conflict. The soldiers who fought in it had to adjust to the particular demands of their theater, from the mud-locked landscape of the Western Front trenches, through the scorching, barren land of the Middle East, to the high-altitude challenges of the Isonzo Front. Wherever they were based, however, all had to endure specific challenges to their day-to-day existence.

◄ British soldiers trudge across the blasted landscape of the Western Front. Battlefield mud not only impeded easy movement, it also began to rot uniform cloth and any equipment made from leather or webbing. Long-term immersion in the mud also accelerated the onset of trench foot.

A WORLD AT ARMS

World War I stands at a crossroads in the history of soldiering. Although the soldier still had the same fundamental priorities as a warrior of the 19th century, technology and logistical advances increased both the scale of operations and the attrition inflicted on the battlefield.

This four-year conflict was a seismic event in European history, which reshaped the map of the world, killed 20 million people, and altered international social and political relations forever. Its roots were complex. A mix of military, economic, imperial, and nationalistic tensions had been building in Europe for decades, and were unleashed by the assassination of Archduke Franz Ferdinand on the streets of Sarajevo, on June 28, 1914.

GLOBAL WAR

It is important to understand why World War I was such a landmark conflict in the history of warfare. True to its name, the war engulfed the planet. The most significant of the

▲ American soldiers about to embark for duty in 1917, with their pets, apparently, coming along for the deployment.

▼ On the Eastern Front, German troops attempt to make a trench more festive by decorating a Christmas tree.

theaters were the Western and Eastern Fronts, the former characterized by landlocked trench warfare, while the latter featured enormous strategic movements by mobile forces. What they shared, however, was a mind-numbing level of human attrition. Outside these primary theaters, fighting was conducted in all manner of places—northern Italy, across the Balkans and the Dardanelles, in Egypt and Mesopotamia, through sub-Saharan Africa, and east to China and certain Pacific islands.

The experience of the soldiers fighting in the war to a large extent depended on their nationality and where they were deployed. Each environment provided its own set of

◄ Private T. P. Loughlin of the 69th Regiment, New York National Guard, 165th Infantry, bids his family farewell before setting off for the front, 1917.

distribution, construction materials, metallurgy and chemistry. In many ways, therefore, the soldiers of World War I could enjoy levels of mobility and logistical support not experienced by previous generations of soldiers.

LETHAL LANDSCAPES

There was a flipside to these advances. The technological revolution also brought machine guns, more powerful and accurate breech-loading artillery, devastating explosives, more efficient small arms, combat aircraft, tanks, and improved communications. In short, the battlefield was now more lethal than ever, a fact that would have a seminal effect on how the soldier lived and the type of kit he carried. So the soldier of World War I lived, and frequently died, in a curious world between primitive landscapes and technological advances.

challenges for both living and fighting, from subzero winter conditions in the Carpathian Mountains to tropical temperatures in East Africa.

INDUSTRIAL WARFARE

Yet in addition to the issues of terrain and climate, the soldiers of World War I were also operating in a time of new technologies. The swift expansion of industrialization in Europe and North America during the 19th and early 20th centuries had brought huge advances in transport (the railroad system, screw-powered, steel-hulled ships, and automobiles), food production and

. . . .

"...stand together. On us of **this generation** has come **the sharpest trial** that has ever **befallen** our race."

DAILY MAIL, AUGUST 1914

. . . .

RIVAL ARMIES

At the outbreak of World War I, the numbers of troops mobilized were highly disproportionate. The Germans, who had been preparing for war, deployed more than 3.5 million men, and France 3 million. Britain, by contrast, fielded an army of just 250,000 professional soldiers. Russia put 5 million men into action, but 400,000 had no weapons.

▼ German soldiers on the Eastern Front, 1916. One of the soldiers had written on a photograph: "My present parlor is...dug four meters deep into the earth, safe from bombs and grenades, but absolutely unprotected against mice, fleas, rats, and lice."

RECRUITMENT AND CONSCRIPTION

As war expanded inexorably, millions of men were drawn from their ordinary and familiar lives and thrust into uniform. Whether they joined up as enthusiastic volunteers or through the official processes of conscription, their lives were changed forever.

A citizen's journey from civilian to uniformed service varied according to the system of recruitment and conscription used by the particular country. Germany, like many continental European countries, operated a system of short-service conscription. This procedure had been refined by the Prussians during the turbulent 19th century, and was essentially copied by France, Austria-Hungary, and Russia.

SHORT-SERVICE CONSCRIPTION

In this conscription system, all eligible civilian males were called up for a brief period of military training and service. Once this was completed, the individual soldier returned to civilian life but remained on a reserve list, to be called up into action again if the country faced a military emergency. The German model provides a good example of how this worked. The recruit would be called up at age 20, as long as his health, family, and social situation allowed. He served full time for two or three years, then went back to civilian life, being recalled three times until he was 45 years old, after which he was no longer eligible. Depending on the level of national emergency, this system allowed a nation to mobilize a huge section of its male population at short notice. In Germany's case, this meant it could go from an army of around 800,000 to one of 3.5 million in just 12 days.

WARTIME POSTERS

Dein Vaterland ist in Gefahr

Melde Dich!

G. KAV. SCHÜTZEN DIV.

Recruitment posters for the combatant countries were a formidable tool for inspiring young men to join up, playing on a mix of patriotism, guilt, panic, and ideas of manliness. Inspiring headlines included "Your country needs YOU!" (Britain), "Who will take this uniform, money, and rifle?" (India), "Your Fatherland is in danger!" (Germany) and "War until Victory!" (Russia). Posters appeared prolifically around the streets, were distributed as flyers and also appeared full page in many national newspapers.

◀ A German soldier leaves his family after receiving mobilization orders in 1914. The call to mobilize was issued on August 1, and the major German attacks in the west began on August 4.

VOLUNTEERS

Britain would also introduce conscription, in early 1916, to maintain its manpower levels. Yet in 1914–15 it had managed to swell its 250,000 regular soldiers by nearly 2.5 million, all of them willing volunteers. Officially volunteers had to be over 19 years old to be eligible for foreign service, but many thousands of much younger men slipped through the net and into uniform. The recruiting offices could scarcely handle the volume; in just one day alone in September 1914 some 33,204 men joined up.

Health issues, however, were a barrier to entry for many men. Flat feet, signs of consumption, heart murmurs—these and other conditions could exclude a man from service. Yet once recruited, the men embarked on about two months of basic training, consisting of

▲ Two soldiers on the concourse of Victoria Station, London, about to leave for the frontline. They are carrying parcels full of food and other provisions from home.

▶ Many British Army volunteers went to war with the 1914-pattern equipment, shown here. Made principally of leather, apart from the canvas haversack and knapsack (6), this featured two ammunition pouches (1 and 2), entrenching tool cover (3), bayonet /bayonet frog and entrenching tool helve (4), and water bottle (5).

marksmanship, physical training (PT) small-unit tactics and bayonet drill. They also had to adjust to hard living, as accommodation consisted of a drafty tent or an improvised billet.

LIFE IN THE TRENCHES

Most combat soldiers actually spent a relatively small proportion of their service life in frontline trenches. Yet the experience of trench life was profoundly difficult at every level, from taking cover from enemy snipers to the basic challenges of staying dry and warm.

Trench warfare was established on virtually all the major European fronts during World War I, but it most characterized the fighting on the Western Front between late 1914 and the spring of 1918. There were typically four types of trench—a frontline trench (or in British-speak "main fire trench") immediately facing the enemy, a support trench a short distance behind, and a reserve trench farther back still, the latter two providing staging posts for men and equipment going up to the front line. Connecting these roughly parallel lines of trenches, and enabling movement between them, were the communication trenches.

HEALTH AND HYGIENE

One common misperception of trench warfare is that the soldier spent his entire service there. In reality, soldiers were typically rotated in a strict pattern every seven or eight days or so, between the frontline, support, and reserve trenches and the rear areas. Rotation

▲ French soldiers in a dugout at Ravin de Souchez, October 1915. Poor conditions for French soldiers contributed to a mutiny in 1917.

▼ Men of the British Border Regiment demonstrate a troglodyte existence in trench dugouts near Thiepval Wood during the Battle of the Somme, August 1916.

frequency could vary dramatically during times of battle or emergency. Yet combat soldiers undoubtedly spent a good part of their year in this unique trench environment.

One of the biggest challenges for a soldier in the trenches was staying clean and dry. During rainy periods, or in places with a high water table, such as Flanders, trenches frequently became either flooded or choked with seemingly bottomless mud. Such conditions led to the skin-eroding syndrome, trench foot, if socks were not changed regularly and boots not dried. In the British forces, soldiers were put into pairs, each responsible for ensuring that the other followed foot protocols.

The mud and earth could be fouled further by human waste—bodies frequently rotted where they had fallen, in and around the trench—and by the inevitable insect life. Lice, for example, plagued an estimated 97 percent of all frontline soldiers. Clothing

FRENCH INFANTRYMAN, 1914

This French soldier wears the "horizon-blue" uniform that came to visually define the French Army during World War I. First issue of the uniform began in part during the fall of 1914, with a general rollout in 1915. The soldier here wears the kepi cap, but in 1915 these were replaced by the Adrian steel helmet, following unacceptable levels of head injury during the early battles.

Uniform
The horizon-blue uniform consisted of a tunic, greatcoat, pantaloons, gaiters, and boots.

Belt kit
On his belt the soldier has two leather ammunition pouches, while on his left hip is a canvas bread bag.

Rifle
The standard rifle of the French soldier was the 8-mm M1886 Lebel.

▲ Trench weapons
Fighting within enemy trenches was a brutal business, delivered in hand-to-hand fashion. All sides therefore fashioned a variety of brutal, medieval-looking trench weapons, including several types of club, three of which are pictured here, together with a viciously spiked knuckle-duster.

> "Filth and rubbish everywhere, **graves** built into the defenses ...**water and muck** on all sides."
>
> WINSTON CHURCHILL, 1915

was periodically immersed in a naphthalene solution, in an attempt to destroy the lice and their eggs. Trench soldiers would also engage in the comradely pastime of "delousing," picking lice off each other's skin and hair and crushing them. Another way to tackle lice impregnation was to run a candle flame along the seams and folds of clothing, where the insects gathered.

ROUTINES AND DANGERS
Between periods of action, trench life was ordered around routines. There would be a morning stand-to, followed by a series of chores such as trench repair, resupply from the support and reserve trenches, sentry duty, food collection, and observation of enemy lines. The routines were punctuated by constant dangers—enemy snipers, trench raids, and the perennial shelling.

▼ Normal life continued to some degree in the trenches. Here a Serbian soldier is being shaved in a trench by one of his comrades.

BEHIND THE FRONT LINE

Life on the front line was by turns terrifyingly violent and incredibly boring, but was always deeply uncomfortable. It is little wonder, therefore, that soldiers longed for their turn to move to the rear areas, where they could get some rest and also seek out entertainment.

Being moved away from the front line usually meant one of three things—you'd been wounded, you were going to the rear areas, or you were on leave.

IN THE REAR

Life in the rear areas was no easy ride. Being still on military duty, soldiers were heavily engaged in manual labor, such as moving ammunition and supplies up to reserve and support trenches, and also in drill and additional training. There were continuing dangers, as long-range artillery could often reach well beyond the lines of trenches. Yet in

▲ This French mobile kitchen would have been ideal for supplying hot, simple food that could be quickly served out behind the front line.

safe areas, being pulled back from the line meant the chance to get clean and well fed. All sides provided communal baths and showers, while those in coastal areas could enjoy a swim in the sea, depending on the season.

There was also the opportunity to indulge in games in leisure time. For German troops, the three-player "skat" was the card game of choice, while the British enjoyed bridge or whist and the Americans poker. Sport was also popular. Football and boxing were the preferred pastimes of many of the European armies, Australian Rules Football for the ANZACS, while other combatants such as the Russians and Ottomans often indulged in various equestrian events or wrestling.

SHOWTIME

Entertainment might also be supplied by external agencies. For American troops, for example, many of these services were provided by Christian or temperance organizations such as

▼ Moroccan Spahis prepare couscous in Ribecourt camp, France. Rear areas were homes to dozens of different microcultures.

AFRICAN-AMERICANS

Some 350,000 African-Americans served in the American Expeditionary Force (AEF) during World War I. Despite giving excellent service, they had to endure prejudice and segregation in the armed services. They weren't allowed to serve at all in the U.S. Marines, and in the Navy and Coast Guard they held only menial positions. Segregation was the norm in the U.S. Army, with two black-only combat divisions formed, the 92nd and 93rd.

the Young Men's Christian Association (YMCA), intent on drawing British and American soldiers away from the twin evils of drink and sex by offering games, spiritual guidance, and movies.

ON LEAVE

Try as they might, no military organization seemed able to keep soldiers away from nightclubs and bars, especially when the men went on leave to a big city, such as Paris for British Empire, French, and American soldiers on the Western Front, or Alexandria for Entente Powers troops in North Africa. Brothels were highly popular. A Canadian General Hospital Report of the war years generally put venereal disease at the top of the list of illnesses contracted among the soldiery. In one listing, a hospital in England recorded having admitted 992 cases of gonorrhea in a seven-month period.

Yet some more salubrious institutions became lifelines for battle-weary soldiers. The British soldiers' club, Talbot House, in the Belgian town of Poperinge, for example, was a renowned haven of rest, comradeship, and food for thousands of homesick men with a perilous future.

RUSSIAN INFANTRYMAN, 1915

This Russian infantryman wears an M1910 sheepskin cap, an M1881 greatcoat, and a leather belt featuring leather M1893 cartridge pouches. The fabric that crisscrosses the chest is the "bashlyk," a warm woollen hood with long tails that could be wrapped around the upper body.

Cartridge pouch
Each pouch held six five-round charger clips for his bolt-action rifle.

Rifle
The standard Russian rifle was the M1891 Mosin-Nagant, a 7.92-mm weapon. Here we see it with the M1891 bayonet.

Greatcoat
The M1881 greatcoat provided heavy protection against the extreme cold. The red collar patches indicate membership of the infantry.

Boots
Regulation boots were black, and made of leather. Russian troops also wore excellent and effective felt overboots during extreme winter conditions.

LIFE ON THE EASTERN FRONT

The experience for soldiers on the Eastern Front was one of extremes, particularly for the Russian forces. While the German Army maintained high levels of cohesion and sustainable logistics, the Russian soldier had to live with scarcity and organizational chaos.

The war on the Eastern Front was fought on a physical scale that dwarfed that of the Western Front. To face the Germans, Russia had mobilized some 6,553,000 men by December 1914. This appears impressive, but the reality was somewhat less so. The army was huge, but millions of the conscripts were the poorest members of society, dragged from hard agricultural labor and often in poor health with no education and extremely little (if any) military training. Coming from a

> "...the **Russian soldiers**...were holding the front **without enough weapons** to go round..."
>
> ARTHUR RANSOME

▼ Russian soldiers write home while serving on the Eastern Front, 1915. Some Russian soldiers might not have home leave for three years.

rigidly hierarchical society, the Russian officers tended to rule their men with brutal disdain. The Russian Army had also generally neglected to develop its officers in the skills of staff work. This actually had a serious impact on the soldiers at the bottom, as important aspects of war management—such as logistics—were often poorly understood. Russian industry also struggled to keep up with demand. For example, of the 6.5 million men mobilized, nearly 2 million went to war without rifles. It is little wonder that Russia suffered such grievous losses during the war. In 1915 alone it took 2 million casualties—dead, wounded, missing, or captured.

VAST DISTANCES

One factor that affected all combatants on the Eastern Front was the physical distances involved across this theater. Although trench warfare was certainly

EYEWITNESS ACCOUNT

British author Arthur Ransome made several visits to the Eastern Front, and described what he witnessed: "I did see a great deal of that long-drawn-out front, and of the men who, ill-armed, ill-supplied, were holding it against an enemy who, even if his anxiety to fight was not greater than the Russians, was infinitely better equipped. I came back to Petrograd full of admiration for the Russian soldiers who were holding the front without enough weapons to go round."

common on the Eastern Front, there were also moments of huge advance and retreat. For the soldiery, this mostly meant epic footslogging across territory more than 1000 miles/1600 km long and hundreds of miles deep. The Russians were, again, particularly badly served in this respect. The Russian road and rail networks were very limited, which not only meant that soldiers had to cover great distances on foot, but also that food and equipment supplies were precarious. Furthermore, because it was hard to transport soldiers to the rear, opportunities for leave were extremely limited, if not nonexistent. Such hard conditions fed into the subsequent political revolution of 1917.

THEATER OF EXTREMES
The Eastern Front was hard on both sides, not least because of terrain and bad weather. During the winter months, armies suffered huge volumes of casualties from frostbite

or hypothermia, especially in high-altitude war zones like the Carpathian Mountains of Romania. Fighting was also brutal: during the period June–September 1916 alone, the Russians lost 1.4 million men, the Central Powers a similar figure.

▲ Russians man a howitzer near Przemysl. Snow and ice could play havoc with a gun's mechanism.

▼ A Russian Army camp in the Carpathian Mountains. This front was cruel for both sides, with freezing temperatures and blizzards.

OVER THE TOP

Although a large part of a soldier's time during World War I was spent waiting for the inevitable release of a major battle, when offensives were unleashed, the experience was typically fearsome and appalling for both the attackers and the defenders.

On the Western Front, the majority of offensive actions between 1915 and spring 1918 were initiated by the Entente Powers, as Britain, France, and later the United States desperately tried to break the deadlock. Notable exceptions include the German assault on Verdun in 1916. As a gloomy rule, such offensives produced grotesque levels of casualties for little geographical advancement.

ARTILLERY BARRAGE

The universal precursor to a major attack was artillery fire. Prior to the British Somme offensive of July 1, 1916, 1,500 British artillery guns delivered an astonishing 1.7 million shells into the German lines over eight days. Artillery fire was carefully scripted in terms of timing, movement, targeting, and volume. Its purposes were to weaken the enemy before the attack, provide a barrier behind which the offensive could advance, and cut enemy defenses to allow unimpeded passage. The effects, however, were less precise. Those caught directly within the blasts would be killed instantly, bodies sometimes vaporizing.

Shrapnel and fragments caused terrible ripping injuries and amputations. The concussive force of the blasts would also cause sickness, diarrhea, disturbed vision, and a host of other physical complaints. Under intense bombardments, men often succumbed to "shell shock"—mental breakdown.

▲ April 1917, Canadian troops attack with bayonets fixed in the expectation of hand-to-hand combat, should they make it across no-man's-land.

◄ Eastern Front, 1914. A German machine-gun team has configured their weapon to deliver indirect-fire, dropping the bullets at a steep angle onto the enemy many hundreds of yards away.

▶ The 9.2-in BL howitzer was one of the heavier "siege" pieces in the British artillery arsenal, and the principal counterbattery equipment of the forces in France. It could deliver a 290-pound/130-kg high-explosive shell to a range of 13,935 yards/12,742 m.

> "I can still see the **bewilderment** and **fear** on the **men's faces** as we went **over the top.**"
>
> HARRY PATCH, BRITISH WWI VETERAN

ACROSS NO-MAN'S-LAND

When the signal to attack was given (usually whistle blasts), the attacking soldiers would have to exit their trenches and attempt to cross no-man's-land into the full force of enemy machine-gun, small-arms, and artillery fire. Depending on the type of soldier, they could be hampered by kit weighing up to 60 pounds/27 kg, making them slow, lumbering targets. The result could be catastrophic levels of casualties. Infamously, on just the first day of the Battle of the Somme, the British suffered nearly 60,000 casualties, 19,240 of them fatalities. What was intended to be a sharp offensive success usually devolved into a long, drawn-out campaign of attrition. The German Verdun offensive, for instance, lasted nearly ten months during 1916. For the soldier, such battles became tragic and prolonged exercises in endurance.

▼ French troops begin an assault in the 2nd Battle of Champagne, September 25, 1915. Note the struggle to move through barbed-wire obstacles.

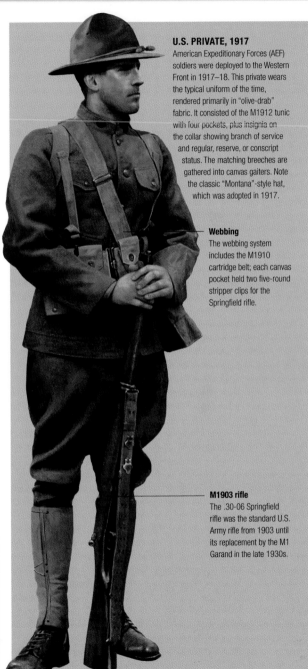

U.S. PRIVATE, 1917
American Expeditionary Forces (AEF) soldiers were deployed to the Western Front in 1917–18. This private wears the typical uniform of the time, rendered primarily in "olive-drab" fabric. It consisted of the M1912 tunic with four pockets, plus insignia on the collar showing branch of service and regular, reserve, or conscript status. The matching breeches are gathered into canvas gaiters. Note the classic "Montana"-style hat, which was adopted in 1917.

Webbing
The webbing system includes the M1910 cartridge belt; each canvas pocket held two five-round stripper clips for the Springfield rifle.

M1903 rifle
The .30-06 Springfield rifle was the standard U.S. Army rifle from 1903 until its replacement by the M1 Garand in the late 1930s.

SPECIALIST SOLDIERS

World War I saw the inexorable rise of the specialist soldier. A combination of technological advances, logistical demands, and the search for tactical advantage spawned dozens of new roles for engineers, signalers, and vehicle crews, among many others.

A telling statistic is that in April 1917, when the United States entered the war, the American Expeditionary Forces (AEF) fielded 3,000 engineers among its personnel. By the time the war ended, just 20 months later, the AEF had deployed 400,000 engineers, such was the inexhaustible demand for technically proficient soldiers.

The requirement for such men was fueled by several factors. First were the advances made in military technology, particularly in the areas of vehicle maintenance (steam and internal combustion engine), signaling and telegraphy, weaponry (especially artillery and automatic weapons, such as machine guns), artillery fire control, and defensive fortification building. These technologies demanded the men to deploy, maintain, and use them. Second, on account of the stalemate of many theaters, commanders increasingly looked to technological solutions to tactical problems.

▲ Scottish troops cross a bridge constructed by British engineers over the Yser River, Belgium. Bridge laying was a major engineering role on both Western and Eastern Fronts.

▼ An essential part of a frontline communication system, this German field telephone was stationed in the Aisne, northern France.

ENGINEERS AND SIGNALERS

In all armies, engineers had wide-ranging importance. In the British forces, for example, the engineer soldier might belong to one of several branches. There was the Royal Army Ordnance Corps (RAOC), Royal Engineers (who also provided Field and Signal companies), Royal Artillery, and Royal Army Service Corps. Between them these formations had responsibilities ranging from managing stocks of ammunition through to maintaining the expanding fleet of military trucks and automobiles. Signals personnel also had the frequently fatal job of laying field telephone cables across the battlefield, but they also engaged in other specialized roles such as message encryption, lamp and flag signaling, and even deploying carrier pigeons. Because of their forward observation roles, signalers often found themselves in isolated positions on the front line, and were extremely vulnerable to shellfire and snipers.

CAPTAIN, ROYAL ENGINEERS

The British Army's Royal Engineers traces its ancestry back to 1717, and in World War I it was one of the major military engineering support arms of the British forces. As well as maintaining railroads, roads, bridges, waterborne logistics, and transport systems, the engineers were also responsible for frontline signaling and communications. By August 1917, the engineers numbered 295,668 men, as opposed to 11,450 in August 1914.

Officer's tunic
Many officers had tunics privately made, so there could be some variation in the cut.

Rank insignia
From 1915 many officers removed cuff insignia in preference for shoulder strap insignia.

Service pistol
From 1915 the Webley Mk VI was a standard British service revolver.

Gaiters
Fabric gaiters served to protect both the pants and footwear from the ingress of mud and water.

Pants
Officer's breeches were often replaced by standard infantry pants during the war.

▲ French sappers dig a tunnel on the Western Front in July 1916. The key dangers of tunneling were roof collapse and also asphyxiation from the buildup of methane or carbon dioxide.

COMBAT ENGINEERS

Engineers were well integrated into combat formations. The Germans and the Austro-Hungarians established engineers in their assault units, tasked with clearing fortifications and other defenses using demolition charges. The British, French, and Germans all deployed combat tunnelers. These were men, usually from civilian mining professions, who would dig deep shafts under the enemy lines, fill them with explosives, then blow the mine up to destroy enemy defenses. It was dark, brutal, and hazardous work. Sometimes German and British tunnels would meet, resulting in grim, subterranean hand-to-hand fighting.

The birth of armored warfare, in the form of early tanks, also produced a need for specialist crews. Life inside a tank was deafening, asphyxiating, and dangerous, but there appears to have been no shortage of manpower.

EXTREME TERRAINS

The global nature of the war meant that governments were deploying and supplying troops in very different geographical territories, with contrasting logistical and tactical demands that themselves shifted according to the time of year.

If we were to select just one example of extreme terrain in World War I, the Isonzo Front instantly suggests itself. For more than two years, the Italians fought the Austro-Hungarians within the precipitous mountain ranges surrounding the Isonzo River, in the Julian Alps on the border between Italy and Austria. Italy's offensive began on these jagged limestone slopes on June 23, 1915, the Italian forces attempting to dislodge the enemy from well-prepared mountain defenses. Logistical and transport issues in the high-altitude terrain meant that supplies of food and ammunition quickly ran low or out—on some occasions the two sides had to resort to throwing rocks at each other—and the wounded lay helpless where they fell, slowly dying from hypothermia with no one to save them.

But this first campaign was just one of 12 major battles and numerous smaller engagements on the Isonzo

Front. As both sides entrenched or tried to outclimb the other, the soldiers were trapped in rocky shelters or caves, at altitudes above 10,000 feet/3000 m, in which they endured hurricane-force winds and freezing temperatures. The Italians even had to build more than 500 electrical overhead cableways, to keep their troops supplied with food, ammunition, and weapons. When attacks took place, soldiers might find themselves scrambling up 1:2 gradient slopes, clinging to the rockface under enemy fire. A full half of the Italian casualties—300,000 of 600,000 men— were taken on this 50 mile/80 km stretch of front.

FROZEN WASTES

The Isonzo Front was not the only high-altitude or subzero landscape of the war. In the Carpathian Mountains, Russian and Austro-Hungarian troops endured temperatures of -25°F/-32°C.

▲ Russians captured by Germans on the Eastern Front c. 1915. Fur, felt, and wool were the best materials for protecting against the dangers of frostbite.

EYEWITNESS ACCOUNT

"We have spent four days in the fire trench. We had only a few casualties. We were put there just after a big attack which has partially failed and the ground between our trench and the Turks were strewn with bodies. It strikes me that they will be there for a long time. In this heat the body and face turn quite black in less than 24 hours and the smell is terrific. The flies—which are myriad—also add to the general discomfort." —Vere Harmsworth, Royal Naval Reserve, Gallipoli, 1915

Boots were stuffed with cardboard and paper in a vain attempt to prevent frostbitten feet. At night, falling asleep in wet clothing or without shelter could result in a man having frozen to death by the morning. The ultimate, if infrequent, horror was the sound of a helpless wounded man screaming as he was attacked by wolves. Across the Eastern Front, throughout each winter, all combatants struggled to survive.

TROPICAL CLIMES

At the opposite extreme were tropical environments, which were no more forgiving. Australian, New Zealand, Indian, and British troops enduring the Gallipoli Campaign had to live under a sweltering sun in primitive trenchlines carved into the Dardanelles coast. The proliferation of insects and lice meant that for most of the campaign, casualties from sickness exceeded

> "I lay in a **filthy stagnant ditch** covered with **mud and slime** from head to foot. I suddenly started to **tremble all over**."
>
> BRUCE BAIRNSFATHER, 1915

▶ Austro-Hungarian troops are pictured at a potable water supply post on the front line of the Isonzo in Italy. During the winter, and at altitude, much effort was expended stopping the water supplies freezing.

casualties from combat. Similarly, in the African theater European forces had to endure the full spectrum of tropical diseases, plus incessant clouds of biting insects. Other hazardous wildlife included snakes, scorpions, crocodiles and hippos. The weather added its own problems—heatstroke during the dry seasons, flash floods during the rains.

FACETS OF WAR: MEDICINE

Battlefield medical treatment has undergone a revolution over the last 100 years. Prior to the 20th century, many medical interventions were positively dangerous, but better understanding of anatomy, hygiene, medicine, and wounds radically transformed soldier survival rates.

Although ancient military medical treatments were certainly basic compared to today, they were not necessarily primitive. The Romans were particularly advanced. Battlefield treatment was provided by *medici* (doctors), *medici ordinarii* (orderlies), and *capsarii* (essentially stretcher bearers), many of these personnel being Greeks. They would generally treat injured soldiers in the field, but over time the Romans also developed large legionary hospitals called *valetudinaria*, where major operations such as limb amputations could take place. These hospitals, located inside fortresses, were generally well-organized affairs, with good sanitation, and they certainly improved the chances of survival, depending on the injury or disease.

GROWING EXPERTISE
Progress in battlefield medical treatment during the medieval and Renaissance periods was slow, although there were individuals who made sage advances in the understanding of wound treatment, such as Frenchman

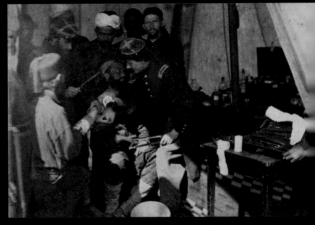

▲ Zouave soldiers in a field hospital tend an injured soldier during the American Civil War, 1863. One of the biggest killers of wounded men at this time was postoperative infection.

▼ A pre-20th century military surgeon's kit, including a bone saw. Amputation levels dropped from the late 19th century with improved vascular treatments.

Ambroise Paré (c.1510 –90) and Englishman Thomas Gale (1507–87). During the 17th–19th centuries, however, military medicine became steadily more professionalized. The British, for example, established permanent regimental surgeons in the 17th century, and during the Napoleonic Wars they also pioneered more effective methods of triage, to distinguish between severity of casualty. Medical advances were also accelerating. During the 19th century, a better understanding of infection control plus the development of anesthetics (1847), X-rays (1897), and vaccinations (especially typhus in 1897) meant that treatment of both illnesses and wounds dramatically improved. (Prior to World War I, disease generally caused more casualties than battle.)

In the 20th century, battlefield medicine truly came of age. Greater scientific understanding of anatomy,

A field hospital during the Boer War, 1899–1902. At some points during this conflict, sickness affected 958 out of every 1,000 troops, with thousands of deaths from cholera, typhus, and dysentery.

▼ A military surgeon removes a bullet from a soldier's arm during World War I. British mobile frontline medical units were known as "Field Ambulances" at this time.

...and plastic surgery (both in World War I), antibiotics (applied militarily from 1939), and improved systems of casualty evacuation, meant that as long as a medic could reach a soldier in time, his chances of survival were respectable.

PROFESSIONAL CARE

Today, such is the efficiency of battlefield evacuation procedures, and the levels of medical skill among military doctors, that wounded soldiers have a 90 percent chance of surviving their injuries if evacuated promptly.

▼ A British Army Medical Emergency Response Team (MERT). aboard a Chinook helicopter.

TIMELINE

1692 The British establish the first mobile field hospitals.

1803 Sickness and disease become the biggest killer of soldiers during the Napoleonic Wars.

1847 The first recorded use of anesthetics in a military context, by a British surgeon to perform a dental extraction.

1854–57 Florence Nightingale's experience of casualty treatment in the Crimean War leads to major British reform of military medical practice.

1897 Transportable X-ray machines are used for the first time during a conflict, the Greco–Turkish War.

1914–18 For the first time in history, mortality from battle exceeds that from disease in a military campaign. Advances in treatments of leg fractures and facial injuries plus improvements in blood transfusions.

1939–45 Soldier survival rates increase dramatically through vaccination programs and the use of antibiotics, especially penicillin and sulphonamides. Motorization improves casualty evacuation times dramatically.

1950 During the Korean War, helicopters are used for the first time for casualty evacuation.

2003 New blood-clotting technologies increase the chances of surviving traumatic amputations.

2003–present Medical advances include bionic limbs for amputees (including types that can be controlled by thought) and ever more rapid evacuation systems.

THE NEW ERA OF WEAPONS

The World War I soldier served at a time when weaponry was increasing in lethality. Not only were personal weapons more powerful, accurate, and quick-firing than ever before, but heavy weapons—artillery and mortars—were reshaping the battlefield.

For soldiers in all armies during the war, the bolt-action rifle would have been their primary weapon. The type was relatively new. Prior to the 1860s, men had gone into action with muzzle-loading muskets, firing about three or four rounds a minute. Now the soldiers had bolt-action rifles like the .303 Short Magazine Lee-Enfield (Britain), the .30-06 M1903 Springfield (America), the 7.92-mm Gewehr 98 (Germany), and the 8-mm Lebel (France). With the rifle's clip- or charger-loaded box magazine and bolt operation, a soldier could now deliver up to 15 aimed rounds per minute, with lethal ranges in excess of 1100 yards/1000 m.

HANDLING

The bolt-action rifles were largely excellent weapons—reliable, hard-hitting, and accurate. In the conditions of life in the field, the soldier would

▲ Three key weapons of the war. 1 The 7.92-mm Mauser Gewehr 98, standard German rifle; 2 the Lewis light machine gun, the best of the LMG types; 3 the .303-in Short Magazine Lee-Enfield (SMLE), the standard British rifle of the war.

▼ A German assault detachment. Note the large numbers of grenades, which were used to clear sections of enemy trench before the attackers entered or moved through them.

nevertheless have spent much time cleaning and maintaining his personal weapon, to ensure that it went on functioning in a crisis. He would, on a daily basis, clean and lightly oil the bolt mechanism, do the same to the bore, and check the wood for cracks and damage. If he looked after his rifle, it would generally look after him.

MACHINE GUNS

The machine gun was in many ways the defining weapon of World War I. There were two basic types. Heavy machine guns (HMGs) like the British Vickers and German Maxim (largely the same weapon), were manned by a small team. One man would fire the gun while others would attend to the ammunition supply and feed, keep the water-coolant system working, and carry the tripod about. Such weapons were real brutes to haul around the battlefield. The total weight of a German MG08 was 58.3 pounds/26 kg just for the basic gun, to which was added a carriage weighing 70.5 pounds/32 kg.

Through the attempt to create more mobile firepower, the conflict also saw the introduction of the light

"Dim, **through** the **misty panes**...as under a green sea, **I saw him** drowning."

WILFRED OWEN, ON A GAS ATTACK

machine gun (LMG) type, such as the American/British Lewis gun and the less successful German MG08/15. These were manned by just one or two men. Unlike the weighty, static HMGs, the LMGs were designed to be carried forward and set up on integral bipods.

NEW THREATS

Artillery was the real killer in World War I, accounting for about 70–80 percent of all casualties. But the soldier also faced new threats. Flamethrowers were used for the first time in World War I, most extensively by the

▲ French soldiers store ammunition out of range of the frontline. The work of moving and stacking thousands of shells was draining.

▼ This British Vickers machine-gun team near Ovillers, July 1916, wear early PH-type antigas helmets. These were impregnated with gas-neutralizing chemicals.

Germans. Poison gas—principally chlorine, mustard gas, and phosgene—was also unleashed, hence soldiers had to become accustomed to wearing a variety of gas protection devices, from early urine-soaked gauze or cloth pads to gas masks with full head protection and a proper filter, such as the British rubberized Small Box Respirator.

UNIFORMS AND KIT

In World War I, out went ostentation and colorful displays of regimental pride, and in came more strictly utilitarian forms of dress, better suited to battlefield conditions.

The move to functional forms of military uniform began back in the late 19th and early 20th centuries, but was still in the process of completion by the time war broke out in 1914. For some armies, and particularly branches of service such as the cavalry, there was a reluctance to relinquish entirely all elements of bravado and color.

REALISM

The French infantry uniform of 1914 is a case in point. At the very beginning of hostilities, the standard French uniform consisted of a Model 1884 red kepi, supplied with a blue cover (not always worn), a blue wool greatcoat and tunic, red pantaloons, leather gaiters, and six-eyelet black boots.

There were several key problems with this kit. First, anything red or brightly colored made you stand out, and so increased your likelihood of being shot. Second, a kepi provided no head protection, as proved by the terrible rates of head injuries during the early months of the war. The French Army therefore quickly dropped red clothing, and helmets were introduced, first in the form of metal skullcaps worn under the kepi, then (more convincingly) as the mild steel Adrian helmet, introduced in 1915.

The uniforms of the other armies showed a similar leaning toward inconspicuous drabness, and steel helmets became standard items. The British adopted the Helmet, Steel, Mk 1, in 1916, and the Germans moved away from their characteristic spiked boiled-leather Pickelhaube in favor of the steel Stahlhelm, also in 1916.

BRITISH INFANTRYMAN SOMME, 1916

This soldier shows the typical appearance of most British infantry during the Somme offensive of 1916. He wears the Pattern 1908 webbing equipment over 1902-pattern tunic and pants, plus the Mk 1 steel helmet that had been introduced in time for the offensive.

Cartridge pouches
In total, the soldier carried up to 150 rifle rounds.

Respirator
The canvas bag contained the Small Box Respirator gas mask.

Rifle
This .303-in SMLE rifle is fitted with the Pattern 1907 bayonet.

Puttees
The woolen puttees extended from the knee to the ankle.

▲ A French Soldier stands in a muddy trench, 1916. Mud and water would rob most uniforms of their insulating properties, leaving the wearer more vulnerable to cold and damp.

EQUIPMENT

Being an infantryman in World War I was a physical burden in terms of weight of kit. One German soldier recalled marching to war in 1914 with 75 pounds/34kg of equipment, and such a weight could increase if soldiers had to carry additional specialist kit, as was common for engineers.

Equipment-carrying systems typically consisted of webbing or leather shoulder straps and belt, to which was attached a backpack, ammunition pouches, bayonet frog, entrenching tool, gas-mask case, map case and pistol (for officers), water bottle and carrier, and additional items such as tent rolls.

There were two main ways of wearing equipment. Using British terminology, there was the "Marching Order," which was essentially the full kit with backpack and all bits and pieces attached. Then there was the "Battle Order," a more streamlined form of kit with the daily-living items removed and the emphasis placed on carrying only combat-essential material, such as ammunition and grenades. Even in Battle Order, however, soldiers could still be lumbering creatures.

GERMAN STORMTROOPER, 1918

The Stormtroopers were specialist German assault soldiers, developed to deliver fast and ruthless offensive action against enemy positions. Their uniform and kit was purposely focused on weaponry and any engineering tools needed for the assault.

Grenades
The chest bags carried multiple grenades for rapid access.

MP18
The 9-mm MP18 "trench broom" was history's first effective submachine gun.

Pants
Stormtroopers sometimes attached leather kneepads to their pants.

Puttees
Puttees not only provided a basic level of waterproofing, they also protected the lower leg from barbed wire and other hazards.

> "The weak must **be chiseled away**... A young German must be as **swift as a greyhound**, as tough as leather, and as **hard as Krupp's steel**."
>
> ADOLF HITLER

WORLD WAR II

1939–45

Although a world war had been fought just two decades before, World War II was a totally different type of conflict. The scale of the theaters, the varieties and lethal nature of weaponry, and the brutality of the fighting reached new levels of intensity. For millions of men and women, World War II was to be the formative experience of their entire lives.

◄ Massed ranks of German soldiers parade for Adolf Hitler in one of the rallies of the 1930s. Membership of Hitler's armed forces gave hundreds of thousands of men an acute sense of purpose and belonging after the desperate years of the global depression, and many were, at least initially, utterly loyal to their leader.

GLOBAL CATASTROPHE

At its heart, World War II was a war of ideologies. Yet for the soldiers who fought in it this became secondary when facing desperate dangers or physical hardships. For them, shelter, ammunition, and comradeship were the chief preoccupations of survival.

◄ Following the disastrous Allied defeat in Western Europe, British servicemen wait at a railroad station for a train to take them home on leave, June 29, 1940.

CASUALTIES

World War II was the deadliest conflict in history. It is estimated that around 60 million people died between 1939 and 1945. The Soviet Union lost 27 million people, and China about 20 million. Germany's losses were 7.3 million, while Britain suffered 450,000 fatalities and the United States 420,000.

In essence, World War II can be studied as the conflation of three geographically distinct conflicts. First, there was the war between Nazi Germany and the Western powers—Britain, the United States, and their allies—fought in Western and Southern Europe, North Africa, the Mediterranean, and the Atlantic. Second, in June 1941 Hitler's armies invaded the Soviet Union, opening an apocalyptic theater of conflict that by 1945 would have cost 3.6 million German and 25 million Soviet lives. Finally, there was the war in the Pacific, initiated by the Japanese attack on the U.S. base at Pearl Harbor on December 7, 1941, and ending with the blasts of the atomic bombs on the cities of Hiroshima and Nagasaki.

NATURE OF WAR

The sheer scale of World War II had a profound effect on the lives of the soldiers who fought in it. A British or Canadian infantryman, for example, might be deployed to France, Burma, or Egypt; an American to Italy or the tropical Pacific; a Russian soldier as far north as the Baltic or as far south as the Crimea; a Japanese soldier might be transported from the barren wastelands of the Chinese steppe to the dense jungles of New Guinea.

The displacement of human beings caused by the war was extensive, and, as in the previous World War, the soldier had to learn quickly how to survive in the new environment. The simple human functions of eating,

> "**I hate war** as only a soldier **who has lived it can**, only as one who has seen its **brutality**, its **futility**, its **stupidity**."
>
> GENERAL DWIGHT D. EISENHOWER

► An injured marine is given plasma on Iwo Jima in 1945. Japanese snipers would often target American medics, knowing their importance.

▼ German prisoners, wrapped in coats, blankets, or anything they could find to protect against the bitter winter weather, are marched through the snowy streets of battered Stalingrad after their defeat by Soviet forces in February 1943.

washing, dressing, and sleeping were rendered complex and sometimes even potentially lethal by in-theater environmental and combat conditions.

IDEOLOGICAL WAR

Soldiers and noncombat staff also had to adjust to the sheer brutality of the conflict. World War II was an ideologically charged conflict, as Nazism, Fascism, Imperialism (British and Japanese), Communism, and Western democracy all vied for power. The struggle was expressed through epic and lengthy battles (Stalingrad alone cost more than 1 million lives), but also devastating casualties among civilian populations. Soldiers became familiar with not only the sights and

sounds of conventional warfare, but also the vast civilian tragedy unfolding around them. For countless millions of soldiers, this was the experience that would haunt them for a lifetime.

World War II was also markedly different from the previous global conflict in its use of weaponry technology and tactics. The two greatest transforming factors in land warfare were armored vehicles and aviation. Combat aircraft alone completely changed the nature of warfare, making soldiers vulnerable to an extra dimension of threat, possibly hundreds of miles from the frontlines. They also had to fight with the understanding that even their homes were potential targets for strategic bombers.

BLITZKRIEG IN EUROPE

The German Wehrmacht achieved its stunning victories in 1939–40 partly through superior equipment and vehicles, but largely through excellent training.

Between September 1939 and June 1940, German forces conquered Poland, Denmark, Norway, Belgium, and France, despite ferocious but futile attempts to stop them. It was an astonishing success, one that underlined the revolution that had taken place in the training of the German soldier.

GERMAN PROFESSIONALISM

There is no doubt that the German soldiers of 1939–40 were the best-trained European military personnel. Under Hitler's leadership from 1933, German militarism had been given full reign, and martial training for German boys began young. At age ten, boys joined the *Deutsches Jungvolk* (German Young People), a youth organization that initiated them into robust outdoor living and group discipline. At 14, matters became more serious when boys transferred to the *Hitlerjugend* (Hitler Youth), which trained the young men in disciplines such as infantry tactics, weapons handling, marching, map reading, vehicle maintenance, and glider flying, all packaged up with brutal physical activity and relentless political indoctrination.

Add a year's physical work in the *Reichsarbeitsdienst* (Reich Labor Service) and three months of basic military training (if he joined the army), and the product was a highly disciplined, tactically aware, and motivated soldier. Note also that the Wehrmacht invested in extremely realistic combat training, resulting in 1–2 percent casualties but producing the "battle innoculation" effects that made a soldier combat-ready.

Sten Mk II
A crude 9-mm submachine gun, the Sten Mk II had a rate of fire of around 500 rpm.

BRITISH INFANTRYMAN
This soldier is wearing the 1940-pattern battledress with the 1937-pattern webbing equipment. Visible kit here includes a water bottle, entrenching tool in carrier, and pack with bedding roll and drinking cup attached.

Water bottle carrier
There were two types of water bottle carrier: the skeleton type shown here, and a full sleeve type.

Boots
The British soldier wore black leather "ammunition boots," also known as Boot, General Service (BGS).

Combined with the German forces' superior technology and tactics, it was little wonder that they were victorious in the opening years of the war.

ALLIED DESPAIR

The Polish and Western European soldiers who faced the German Army had roughly the same levels of personal firepower and equivalent levels of kit and uniform. The same level of professionalism, however, was often lacking. The British introduced conscription in peacetime, on April 27, 1939, but many of the men who joined up had rudimentary training that ill prepared them for the fast-moving war. France had a huge land army, but was outclassed by German innovation and daring.

▼ The Polish armed forces in 1939 still contained a significant number of traditional horse-mounted cavalry. Although the soldiers retained the cavalry saber, and on occasion some troopers did revert to lance attacks, the classic cavalryman's lance had largely been replaced by carbine rifles. Against German automatic weapons, the Polish cavalry took inevitable heavy losses.

Stahlhelm (steel helmet)
The highly recognizable German steel helmet was introduced in 1935.

GERMAN INFANTRYMAN
The German infantryman of 1940 had a high standard of uniform and kit. He wears the field gray M40 tunic and matching pants tucked into the *Marschstiefel* (marching boots). On his belt are ten-round 7.92-mm ammunition pouches, and the ever-useful *Zeltbahn* pup tent is worn on the back.

Equipment
The soldier's equipment was supported by a webbing system that consisted of a leather (later canvas) waist belt with Y-straps running over the shoulders.

Marching boots
The German Army was almost unique in having a pull-on boot as standard. They were given the nickname *Knobelbecher* (dice shakers) by the soldiers.

CAMPAIGNING IN NORTH AFRICA

The campaign in the scorching landscape of North Africa in 1940–43 was a trial for body, mind and equipment. Regardless of the opposing soldiers' training or motivation, the environmental conditions affected all sides equally.

The war in North Africa ran from 1940, with the Italian invasion of Egypt in September, through to 1943, when German forces were finally expelled from the continent via Tunisia. It was a hard-fought, highly mobile campaign, seesawing across the top of Africa as each side experienced advance and retreat. This movement to a large extent defined experience on the ground. Soldiers spent hours on the move by vehicle or foot under terrible heat, but as soon as they stopped they would have to spend equal hours digging defensive positions into rock-hard desert soil. It was common for soldiers to pass out under the effort, or to succumb to potentially lethal heat exhaustion. Much of the physical work had to be done at night.

CONDITIONS

With heat came a whole host of associated challenges, experienced by Italian, German, British, American, Australian, and New Zealand soldiers alike. Dust penetrated everything—tents and vehicles, food and drinking

▲ Men of the British Army's Long Range Desert Group (the forerunner of the SAS) returning from a three-month trip behind enemy lines. Note how they have adopted Arab headdress, which provided excellent protection from the sun for the scalp and neck.

◀ The New Zealand crew of this American-made Sherman tank, operating with the British Eighth Army in the Western Desert, takes a much-needed rest after 60 hours of continuous fighting. Under the desert sun, tanks often had internal temperatures of 122°F/50°C.

water (producing aggravated stomach complaints), and eyes. The combination of dust and heat produced "desert sores," open wounds on the skin that often became infected. Much time was spent on vehicles—the dust clogged air filters and polluted fuel. There was also the problem of flies, which hunted in endless clouds for any scrap of moisture, gathering around mouths, food, water bottles, and latrines, resulting in dysentery being a common blight.

COMBAT

The desert regions of North Africa were a unique environment for warfare. Being mostly flat, there was

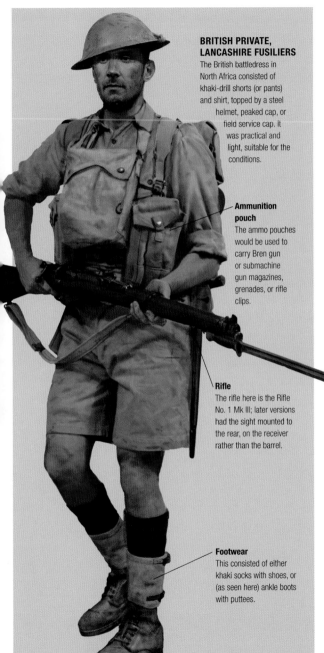

BRITISH PRIVATE, LANCASHIRE FUSILIERS
The British battledress in North Africa consisted of khaki-drill shorts (or pants) and shirt, topped by a steel helmet, peaked cap, or field service cap. It was practical and light, suitable for the conditions.

Ammunition pouch
The ammo pouches would be used to carry Bren gun or submachine gun magazines, grenades, or rifle clips.

Rifle
The rifle here is the Rifle No. 1 Mk III; later versions had the sight mounted to the rear, on the receiver rather than the barrel.

Footwear
This consisted of either khaki socks with shoes, or (as seen here) ankle boots with puttees.

"A shabby, gritty landscape. The sweat oozes and trickles all day. This is war..."

LT NEIL MCCALLUM, 51ST HIGHLANDERS

little by way of cover. Soldiers largely had to rely on digging little more than scrape holes for themselves, and then improvise overhead cover with camouflage netting, which gave little real protection. Travel by truck could be especially perilous, as the inevitable dust cloud behind the vehicle provided a convenient visual signpost for predatory enemy ground-attack aircraft.

Hundreds of thousands of Axis soldiers were taken prisoner during the North African campaign. Conditions in local POW camps were spartan, but for some prisoners capture meant a new life. Some 130,000 Italian POWs, for example, were sent to camps in Britain, and many remained there after the war.

▼ This German propaganda photo depicts soldiers baking bread in Mersa Matruh, Egypt, November 1942. By this time in the war, German logistics were collapsing in the theater, and food supplies were often very scarce for frontline troops.

ARMOR AND MECHANIZATION

World War II was a mechanized conflict. Armored vehicles became the "tip of the spear" for most armies, while entire fleets of trucks and light vehicles provided logistical reach. The life of a vehicle crewman, however, was tough and unrelenting.

It might appear that men who operated inside armored vehicles had a safer and easier life than infantry troops on the outside. Nothing could be farther from the truth. Armored vehicles were primary targets for enemy antitank guns, tank-hunting teams, ground-attack aircraft, and other tanks, resulting in appalling casualty rates. The U.S. 3rd Armored Division went into combat in Normandy with 232 M4 Sherman tanks, but by the end of the campaign (when we include replacement vehicles) had suffered 648 tanks destroyed and another 700 immobilized but repaired. During the whole war, the Red Army lost about 96,500 tanks and self-propelled guns, or around 70 percent of its entire stock.

The human story behind these figures is thousands of young men blown apart or burned alive in their

vehicles. Life was anything but safe under armor, and combat stress casualties were also high.

CLOSE QUARTERS

Compounding the issues of violent combat was the general experience of operating an armored vehicle. As an example, take the Panzer Mk IV, one of the mainstay German tanks of the war.

◀ Examples of German divisional vehicle insignia. These designs, and many others like them, were displayed on the vehicles' hulls and mudguards. Other markings (on armored vehicles) would include a chassis number (although this was often overpainted in action), tactical markings (which designated the vehicle's role) and a three-digit vehicle number, which defined the vehicle's company, platoon, and position with the platoon.

▼ Red Army T-34 tanks spearhead an attack against German positions. Note how the accompanying infantry use the tanks both for cover and for a quick ride to the battle front. Tank crews had to cooperate closely with friendly infantry at all times.

> "**A tank** with its hatches closed was **like a blind monster** at the mercy of a fast, **sharp-eyed enemy**."
>
> PETER ELSTOB, BRITISH TANK CREWMAN

It had a five-man crew: commander, gunner, loader, driver, radio operator/bow machine-gunner. Each man had heavy responsibilities, and had to cope with the psychological pressure of being confined with other crew members for weeks at a time. With the hatches shut for combat, the interior was dark and claustrophic, adding the anxiety of having no visual connection with the outside world. During action, the vehicle stank of engine fumes, gun propellant, and body odor, and there would be constant sounds of small-arms ammunition clanging off the outer hull. Occasionally, there would be a huge bang as an antitank shell glanced off the turret. Vibration induced headaches and visual disturbances.

▲ A German tank commander sits in the turret of his Panzer IV. Before the war, the tactical intention had been for the commander to sit in the open turret and provide guidance to the crew inside. However, it was quickly discovered that life on the outside was perilous, and the commander retreated back inside.

from enemy ground troops (although not aircraft), and might also enjoy ancilliary benefits such as good food and long rest periods. Life was very different for truck drivers in frontline areas. Countless hours would be spent conducting field maintenance on the vehicles in ill-lit improvised workshops. The shifts were relentless during a major campaign, and at the pickup and dropoff areas the soldiers were often involved with the back-breaking task of loading or unloading. Like tanks, a frontline truck was a tempting target to enemy forces, but without the protective armor.

OTHER VEHICLE CREWS

Those who manned trucks or other "soft-skinned" vehicles might have an easier life. For example, a British staff car driver, ferrying a general around the rear areas, would usually be safe

▶ A German motorized column takes a break. The vast distances of the Eastern Front placed a great mechanical burden on overworked vehicles, so crews were constantly conducting maintenance and repair duties.

APOCALYPSE—THE EASTERN FRONT

The war on the Eastern Front reached an unimaginable scale. For the millions of soldiers on the front line, life expectancy could be measured in weeks, if not days, and German brutality toward the Soviet civilian population and Red Army prisoners was extreme.

The Soviet Army, despite numbering about 3 million men in 1941, was woefully ill prepared for the German invasion of June 1941. Political purges of some 35,000 officers from the Red Army in 1937 and 1938 had left the leadership terribly weakened, and this showed in the catastrophic collapse of the Soviet defense in 1941—in one battle alone, at Kiev in September, the Germans took 600,000 Soviet prisoners.

SURVIVOR

Despite the Red Army's tactical and strategic failures, from which it recovered, there was no doubting the resilience of its average soldier. With some 180 ethnic groups under the Soviet umbrella, the backgrounds of "average" soldiers were incredibly diverse, from men living in cosmopolitan western

cities such as Leningrad, through to hardy landworkers from Asiatic Siberia. Most were physically tough individuals, however, having been raised in a generally poor society

▲ A German machine-gun crew in action on the Eastern Front, 1943. One man operates the gun itself, while his assistant ensures the smooth feed of ammunition belts.

EYEWITNESS ACCOUNT

"Now there is an impassable obstruction on the roads, on the army's supply route. Everyone becomes infected with uncontrollable fury. Everyone shouts at everyone else. Sweating, swearing, mud-spattered men start laying into sweating, shivering, mud-caked horses that are already frothing at the mouth... The scene is repeated a hundred times a day with monotonous regularity. But by evening there has been progression of twelve, six, occasionally only three miles."

—German soldier Peter Bamm

GERMAN PANZERGRENADIER, 1944

By 1944, the uniforms of German troops on the Eastern Front had largely improved in design, although there was often some deterioration in the quality of materials used in manufacture.

MP40

The 9mm MP40 was the standard submachine gun of the German Army.

Magazine pouches

Equipped purely for combat, this soldier has two three-cell magazine pouches, each pouch holding a 32-round magazine.

Zeltbahn

The Zeltbahn pup tent could be used as a tent but was also worn belted as a form of camouflage poncho.

based on hard physical labor on the land or in factories. Pay was poor, training inadequate, equipment was basic in the extreme (many soldiers had no rifles at the beginning of the war), mechanization was incomplete (meaning they walked everywhere), and communist political scrutiny was constant, thanks to embedded political officers within the units.

GERMAN VULNERABILITIES

The German soldier, at the beginning of the conflict, was militarily superior in many ways to the Soviet man, at least in terms of soldiering skills. But the Eastern Front was a daunting theater for the Germans, totally unlike Western Europe. Distances were far greater, resulting in major logistical problems and the psychological issues of remote objectives—soldiers often reported feeling demoralized at traveling for weeks toward a constantly retreating horizon. The scale of the fighting was greater—more than 800,000 Germans were lost in 1941 alone—meaning that small units experienced higher levels of personal loss. It was clear in this theater that the war was a fight to the death.

▼ Russian prisoners of war on the Eastern Front. Out of about 5.7 million Soviets taken prisoner, some 3.3 million died of mistreatment, starvation, or execution.

SURVIVING THE SOVIET WINTER

The Soviet winter was familiar to the Red Army, but to the German forces it was the most appalling shock when it hit them in 1941–42. At first, in the struggle to survive, the winter conditions caused even more casualties than the fighting.

The winter on the Eastern Front, when it finally descended in November 1941, nearly paralyzed the entire German Army. Temperatures plunged to -40°F/-40°C, snow piled up many feet in depth, blizzards swept the roads and fields. The German soldiers had almost no specialist winter clothing, and tens of thousands succumbed to either frostbite or hypothermia. Certain items of uniform and equipment were revealed as fatally flawed. The German jackboot, for example, conducted heat away from the feet via the hobnail studs on the bottom. Logistics broke down as virtually the entire German fleet of nonwinterized vehicles froze solid, including the fuel in the tanks, or their batteries lost all power, restored only by measures such as lighting a fire beneath the engine. The German Fourth Army received a food consignment that consisted of only frost-fractured bottles of wine. Weapons also locked solid. While the Red Army had mastered subzero weapon lubrication (often using a mix of kerosene and axle grease), the German oils froze around moving parts such as bolts and triggers.

> "The **weather suddenly broke** and almost overnight the **full fury** of the **Russian winter** was upon us."
>
> GENERAL BLUMENTRITT

Gewehr 43
The Gew 43 was a semiautomatic rifle, here fitted with an optical sight.

Warm clothing
Under the parka, the soldier wore the M36 German issue woolen sweater.

Pants
The camouflaged white winter pants were often worn over M1943 field pants.

GERMAN SNIPER, 1945
This soldier illustrates how much German winter clothing had improved by the late years of the war. He wears a waterproof parka coat; some versions were reversible, white on the outside for winter and woodland/splinter camouflaged or field gray on the inside. Matching pants complete the outfit. Gone are the jackboots, replaced with proper insulated boots, possibly taken from a dead Soviet soldier (a common practice).

◄ Marching through the ever-deepening snows in single file, Russian soldiers trudge toward Stalingrad. As well as thick greatcoats, many also donned the excellent *telogreika* quilted suit.

MASTERING THE COLD

It would be wrong to present the Red Army soldiers as totally comfortable with their winters, but they were certainly better prepared. Vehicles and small arms were designed from the outset for winter conditions, and the Red Army soldier enjoyed decent winter clothing, such as the fur *ushanka* hat and compressed felt overboots (*valenki*), the latter going a long way to preventing frostbitten toes. Many troops were also expert at building warm improvised shelters lined with pine branches. By the second winter of the war, however, the Germans had learned many lessons and were also better equipped for the cold.

▲ January 1943: A German soldier endures the freezing cold in an isolated machine-gun post dug into the snow on the Eastern Front. The soldier would need to keep moving almost constantly to avoid frostbite and hypothermia.

RASPUTITSA

Fall rains and the spring thaw bought new problems for both German and Russian soldiers. Known as the *rasputitsa* (quagmire season), it turned earth tracks and fields into impassable oceans of mud. It could take hours to move a single mile, and boots and clothing were rotted by the mud.

HORSE POWER

The Wehrmacht still relied heavily on horses for logistics, despite their vehicles. Many German horses were taken from comfortable pastures in Germany to short and horrific lives of overwork and freezing conditions on the Eastern Front. In just two months, December 1941 and January 1942, the German forces lost 179,000 horses.

◄ German enlisted men insignia. The bottom three rows show (from bottom to top) camouflaged clothing arm patches, shoulder straps, and collar patches for (from right to left) corporal, sergeant (engineers), senior sergeant (motor recce), sergeant-major (Panzer grenadiers), and staff sergeant (Panzers) ranks. The three top rows show (again from right to left) private, private 1st class, lance-corporal, senior lance corporal, and staff lance-corporal infantry ranks.

AIRBORNE FORCES

Although airborne troops were established in earnest in the 1930s, it was only in World War II that this unique type of soldier became an operational practicality. Trained to perfection for risky missions, airborne troops were a true elite within an army.

The leaders in the development of airborne soldiers—that is, soldiers capable of deploying by either parachute or landing aircraft—were the Russians and the Italians during the 1930s. These early paratroopers had nerves of steel—there are photos of Russian paratroopers sliding off the wings of transport aircraft to make a jump. Yet it was the Germans who would turn the concept into an operational reality, with the development of the Fallschirmjäger.

GERMAN PARATROOPERS

Airborne forces were first formed within the Luftwaffe and Heer (German Army) in 1936. By 1940, they were ready to conduct operations, which they did to startling effect in Norway, the Netherlands, and Belgium. The landmark early operation was the capture of the Belgian Eben Emael fortress on May 10–11, by a small force deployed by glider onto the roof of the defenses. Only with the airborne invasion of Crete in May 1941, in which the Fallschirmjäger suffered unacceptable losses, were the paras converted to elite ground infantry.

Until 1943 the Fallschirmjäger were all volunteers, many already serving military personnel. They embarked on a physically and mentally arduous training regime. A typical program was eight weeks of punishing physical and tactical training at Stendal, followed by a 16-day parachute course. If they

STATIC-LINE JUMPS

In a static-line drop, each soldier fastened a ripcord line to a wire inside the jump aircraft. The ripcord would deploy the parachute automatically after a predetermined drop distance, meaning the paras would land close together if they all jumped in quick succession.

▼ German paratroopers, May 1941, wearing parachute smocks. The man second right is wearing kapok-filled canvas knee protectors.

▲ British airborne soldiers inspect their static-line connections prior to a jump. The British parachute design meant that they would jump feet-first out of the aircraft, whereas the German design necessitated an unnerving head-first deployment.

made six drops successfully, they were awarded the coveted paratrooper's badge. The German para had to get used to a hair-raising deployment method, dropped from around 330 feet/100 m, with RZ 1 and RZ 16 parachutes that gave them almost no control over descent and landing direction. Plus they had to jump unarmed—weapons were dropped separately in containers.

ALLIED PARATROOPERS

British and American paratroop forces began formation in the early years of the war, and full-blown airborne divisions were at the vanguard of the D-Day landings in June 1944 and the huge airborne Market Garden operation at Arnhem. American and British training was as tough as the German equivalent. Yet the Allied parachutes, by 1944, allowed a good degree of control over descent direction and speed, and soldiers could also carry small arms and grenades, so they were ready to fight as soon as they landed. American paras also received extra pay, although glider troops did not—a source of tension in the ranks.

U.S. PARATROOPER, D-DAY, JUNE 1944
This para of the 501st Parachute Infantry Regiment (PIR) is wearing the M42 jump suit with reinforced lower leg sections. On his chest he has an M16 smoke grenade and a Mk II fragmentation grenade.

M1 Garand
The .30-cal M1 Garand was an eight-shot semiauto rifle.

Webbing
Paratroopers would carry limited kit into combat, focusing on ammunition, water, comms equipment, first-aid packs, and maps.

Jump boots
The lace-up "Corcoran" jump boots were designed by the Corcoran and Matterhorn Company specifically for U.S. paratroopers.

THE U.S. ARMY AND MARINES

In 1939, the United States had one of the world's smallest armies. Yet the spread of war through Europe, then the American entry into the conflict in 1941, transformed the U.S. Army and Marine Corps into strategically powerful and professional fighting forces.

In the autumn of 1940, with war spreading out from Europe, the United States Congress enacted a national draft by lottery. Suddenly hundreds of thousands of American men became eligible for a year's military service; after the Japanese attack on Pearl Harbor on December 7, 1941, the period of service was extended to the duration of the war plus six months.

The period of basic training for a soldier or Marine differed according to branch of service and the period of the war, but typically (following Pearl Harbor) lasted 6–10 weeks and covered familiar ground: military etiquette, rifle marksmanship and small-arms training, bayonet training, close-order drill, field survival and combat skills, plus lots of physical fitness, including runs of increasing distance with full kit. The purpose of the training was to build a generation of physically strong and militarily cohesive young men.

▲ African-American and white troops wait in a chow line at basic training, 1940.

▼ June 1944: American assault troops and equipment land on Omaha Beach, Normandy. At this most contested of landing areas, the American forces suffered a total of 2,400 casualties.

KIT AND EQUIPMENT

The U.S. Army and Marine Corps would go on to have some of the best weapons and equipment of the war, but it took time for standardization to embed itself. The U.S. Marine Corps actually prided itself on having older and more basic equipment than the U.S. Army. So while the U.S. Army soldier was mostly

U.S. ARMY RATIONS

The two classic types of field ration for U.S. soldiers were the K rations and C rations. K rations were a daily ration introduced in 1942. They consisted of a single box in which were packaged three separate meals: breakfast, dinner, and supper. C rations were canned foods for frequent use, with six 12-ounce cans providing complete daily nutrition. Often the labels peeled off the cans, making the identity of the meal unknown until the can was opened.

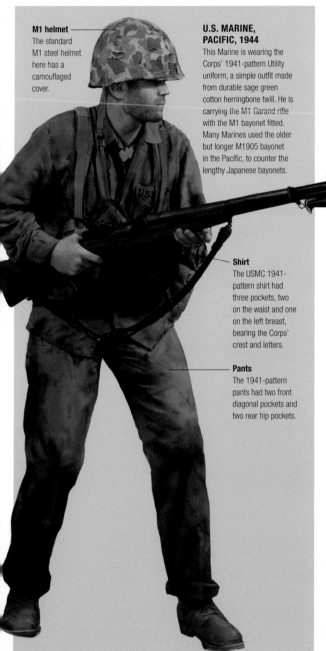

M1 helmet
The standard M1 steel helmet here has a camouflaged cover.

U.S. MARINE, PACIFIC, 1944
This Marine is wearing the Corps' 1941-pattern Utility uniform, a simple outfit made from durable sage green cotton herringbone twill. He is carrying the M1 Garand rifle with the M1 bayonet fitted. Many Marines used the older but longer M1905 bayonet in the Pacific, to counter the lengthy Japanese bayonets.

Shirt
The USMC 1941-pattern shirt had three pockets, two on the waist and one on the left breast, bearing the Corps' crest and letters.

Pants
The 1941-pattern pants had two front diagonal pockets and two rear hip pockets.

> # "I love the infantry because they are the underdogs."
>
> U.S. JOURNALIST ERNIE PYLE

equipped with the modern semiauto M1 Garand rifle from the late 1930s, it took the Marine Corps until November 1941 to swap out their bolt-action M1903 Springfields for the new M1. Both services had similar, quite basic, uniforms—shirt and pants, M1928 cartridge belt, M1928 haversack, and the classic M1 steel helmet, which also worked as a cooking pot, wash basin, latrine, and improvised entrenching tool.

DEPLOYMENT
The experience of the soldier or Marine depended very much on where he was posted. Life on the front line was invariably hard. Italy, for example, was held as a dream posting until soldiers were actually sent there, to survive under the torrential seasonal rains and through terrible mountain battles. Marines and soldiers in the Pacific lived mostly in spartan island bases or on troopships. Because of the vast distances involved in that theater, the options for leave were poor, although one-month trips back home or a short vacation in Hawaii were given. Soldiers in Western Europe, particularly those in pre-D-Day England, could experience greater levels of luxury and entertainment. Many American soldiers posted to Britain found love there—some 100,000 GI brides went back to the United States after the war, as did an estimated 150,000–200,000 women from mainland Europe. In tragic balance, however, nearly 400,000 Americans did not survive the war.

THE JAPANESE SOLDIER

The life of a Japanese soldier was hard from the first day he entered basic training. Treatment from NCOs and officers was frequently cruel, and equipment and rations were basic.

To understand the Japanese soldier, ideological context is critical. Japanese society during the 1920s and 1930s had fused nationalistic militarism with a corruption of the samurai *bushido* warrior code and the implicit emperor worship that prevailed among the Japanese population. These values were hammered into cadets and recruits constantly, through a training program that bordered on the sadistic. The result was a soldier given to blind obedience to superiors, a contempt for the enemy, and a general acceptance that death was preferable to surrender.

SPARTAN LIVING

On the front lines, the Japanese soldier lived in conditions of austerity unthinkable to most Western armies. Food tended to be dull and unvarying—rice, dried fish, and simple vegetables, with occasional treats such as crabmeat, plums, and canned clams. In the Pacific combat zones, particularly once United States air and naval power began to interdict Japanese supply lines, daily nutrition might be little above starvation levels.

There were some concessions to keeping up the soldier's spirits. Morale boosters came in the form of *imon bukuro* (comfort bags)—packets containing confectionery, toothbrush and paste, socks, toilet paper, and other "luxuries" sent by considerate women back in Japan. The womenfolk would also produce *senninbari*, or the "belt of 1,000 stitches," typically worn around the waist and intended as an amulet to ward off harm. As experience would show, this did little good.

JAPANESE PRIVATE, MALAYA, 1941
The soldier here is wearing the M98 field service uniform, consisting simply of a single-breasted tunic with a stand-and-fall collar, and long pants with puttees and tapes. His field cap features a practical neck protector, useful in the tropical climate of the region.

Ammunition pouches
Two leather ammunition boxes are worn on the front of the belt, each holding 30 rounds.

Rifle
The rifle is the underpowered 6.5-mm Arisaka Type 38, of which 3.4 million were produced during the war.

Puttees
Protecting the lower legs are puttee wraps, with khaki tying tapes forming the characteristic X shape at the front of the leg.

COMBAT CONDITIONS

As surrender was considered anathema to the Japanese, they would often fight with ferocious stubborness to the death. During the battle for Iwo Jima, of the 21,000 Japanese soldiers on the island, over 18,000 were killed and only 216 were taken prisoner.

Contrary to popular mythology among the Allies, the Japanese soldier was no more at home in the jungles of Southeast Asia than British, American, Australian, New Zealand, or other soldiers. Casualties from illnesses such as malaria and cholera still ran unacceptably high among the Japanese ranks, as did the effects of heat exhaustion. What the Japanese did have, however, was formidable endurance, a familiarity with physical hardship, and an undoubted ability at tactical improvisation. During the Malayan campaign of 1941–42

▲ Showing the legendary toughness of the Japanese Army, military engineers support a temporary bridge for soldiers to cross a river while marching through Malaysia.

thousands of Japanese troops used bicycles to advance quickly down the peninsula to outpace the British, even riding on the wheel rims when the rubber tires were blown. Yet Japanese weaponry was largely inferior to that of the Allies, a key factor in limiting the casualties they imposed on their enemy.

► U.S. Marines take a Japanese prisoner on Tinian island, 1944. Japanese resistance was so ferocious that many U.S. soldiers refused to accept prisoners.

Propaganda has always been an integral component of conflict. Soldiers are both the targets and the producers of propaganda, as each side seeks either to bolster their own morale or deflate that of their opponents, and maintain the support of civilians at home.

▲ The Arch of Titus in Rome, built around 82BC, was a permanent monument to the military victories of the Roman Emperor Titus.

Military applications of propaganda have always been with us. Ever since a Greek or Roman commander commissioned a piece of triumphal statuary or architecture, powerful interests have used propaganda to control and guide public perception. The word was only coined in the 17th century, however, and prior to the 20th century it was mainly confined to basic print media and to song traditions. It was in the 20th century that propaganda really gained power.

MASS CONTROL
Propaganda touched the common soldier in many ways in the 20th century, but we might loosely categorize these ways as positive and negative. On the positive side were the attempts, across both World Wars, to encourage recruitment and to improve morale. Recruitment posters were artistically and conceptually powerful. The British in World War I were given images and straplines that equated enlisting with manliness and courage. One poster read: "There are three types of men: Those who hear the call and obey. Those who delay. And— the others." Similarly, Nazi Germany used epic artwork to give its men and soldiery a sense of destiny and a belief in the power of pure will, although this belief was progressively eroded as the war turned against Germany.

MANIPULATION
But the combatants in the World Wars have also used propaganda as a weapon against their enemies. U.S. servicemen in the Pacific frequently tuned their radios to "Tokyo Rose," beguiling

▶ An early communist propaganda vehicle, decked out with newspapers, posters, and a phonograph, is manned by Red Army political soldiers.

1. Schutzstaffel-Appell
der Gruppe Oft in Berlin
11., 12., 13. August

Japanese female voices that explained, in seductive tones, why the Americans were losing the war. (The main voice was provided by U.S. citizen Iva Toguri, who was arrested and convicted of treason after the war.) The broadcasts could certainly be unnerving, at times, mentioning specific names of men and units, and their exact locations. However, it seems that on the whole Tokyo Rose was popular for the laughability of the broadcasts.

Other tools of propaganda were more basic. Russian political officers would sometimes make threatening broadcasts through loud speakers to German troops on the Eastern Front, telling them to surrender or suffer the consequences. In the absence of any response, Russian artillery would then pound the German lines for a short time, before the broadcasts began again. Leaflets were also dropped in their millions. One poster deposited on Allied troops by the Germans showed the sad face of a young woman, beneath which lies the corpse of a U.S. soldier. The text, designed to fill the

◄ Nazi recruitment posters focused on the heroic nature of military service. Note the perspective—the viewer always looks up to the soldier and the swastika.

▼ U.S. Army soldiers distribute copies of the official newspaper of the 1st Armored Division, *Baghdad Now*, in Iraq in 2004. The soldiers are from the 315th Tactical PSYOPS (Psychological Operations) Company.

soldier with a longing for home, reads poignantly: "Waiting—in vain."

Propaganda since World War II has largely been less egregious, but the "psyops" war is still prosecuted with vigor. Newspapers, magazines, and social media are used to present the preferred political slant of armies and governments. At the time of writing, the insurgent group Islamic State or IS has had huge success in its online recruitment campaign, which purports to show IS victories and appeals to sensationalists through brutal images.

FORGOTTEN WARS IN THE EAST

While the fighting in Western Europe, Italy, and the Pacific islands drew considerable public attention, long-running and bitter campaigns such as those in Burma and New Guinea were often overlooked, despite the human challenges they posed.

One characteristic of the campaigns in New Guinea and Burma was their longevity. The New Guinea campaign, which sucked in American, Australian, New Zealand, Dutch and British forces, ran from January 1942 until the very end of the war in August 1945. The Burma war (the only eastern theater in which the British were the majority Allied force) had an almost identical time frame.

LIFE IN THE JUNGLE

So it was that thousands of men were taken from familiar lives in developed towns and cities, and thrust into an almost prehistoric wilderness for many months, if not years. The men who fought in these theaters had to

▶ British Chindits traveling through the jungle. The Burmese interior was largely inaccessible to vehicles, so mules were the best mode of logistics.

▼ Health and hygiene were critical to surviving the jungle conditions. Here a soldier receives basic dental treatment in New Guinea, 1942.

learn quickly the ways of the jungle. Some, such as Orde Wingate's famous "Chindits" and the American "Merrill's Marauders," became deep-penetration jungle-warfare specialists in Burma, much feared by the Japanese.

Combat was frequent in these theaters, often conducted at close quarters, with the jungle foliage limiting visibility. Being wounded was a desperate fate—during long-range operations, many men had to be left to their fate in a jungle clearing, the rest of the unit unable to carry the man through the unforgiving landscape.

Indeed, the landscape was like an enemy in itself. The hot, humid climate produced legions of heat exhaustion casualties, and rotted leather

VERA IN BURMA

The British "forces sweetheart" Vera Lynn traveled through the war zones entertaining the Allied troops. She also went to Burma in 1944 (part of a three-month tour of the Far East), an inhospitable and inaccessible theater that many entertainers avoided. By so doing, she provided the troops there with a huge morale boost, as many felt forgotten by the British public.

or webbing equipment quickly. The vegetation acted as a dense obstacle to efficient movement and navigation. If a soldier tripped and fell, he knew it was better not to reach out and grab a branch, as that action would often result in thorn-lacerated hands. During the monsoons, the jungle floor became a quagmire, and flash floods and mudslides were lethal seasonal hazards.

DISEASE

Yet the biggest problem was disease. The endless, whining clouds of mosquitoes brought with them malaria. In 1943 in Burma, a total of 84 percent of manpower was afflicted by the disease; for every soldier wounded in action, 120 would be sick from disease. The crisis was limited by fresh measures implemented when Lieutenant-General William Slim took over as commander of the Fourteenth Army. New insecticides and repellents were introduced, and better clothing protocols (such as no shorts allowed and shirt sleeves rolled down after dusk). These measures meant that malaria was under control by 1944.

▼ New Guinea, 1943. Australian soldiers take a break from operations. NCOs had to ensure that men stayed properly hydrated throughout operations.

AUSTRALIAN INFANTRYMAN, NEW GUINEA 1943

This infantryman has the defining Australian bush hat, highly practical in tropical climes. The rest of his uniform and equipment is composed of a mix of British and U.S. items.

Webbing

The webbing is the standard British 1937 pattern, with two large ammunition pouches at the front.

M1 Thompson

The M1 Thompson was a United States-produced submachine gun, firing the powerful .45-caliber cartridge.

Battledress

The Australians developed their own form of jungle battledress, although later in the war they also used large amounts of American clothing.

Gaiters

These canvas gaiters protected the soldier's ankles and boots. The jungle environment was very hard on boots, rotting leather and canvas.

ENDGAME IN EUROPE

As the noose tightened around the Third Reich in 1944–45, the fighting intensified on many fronts. The critical focus for soldiers in all armies became simply to survive until the war was over, when they could think about peacetime lives.

The German Army of late 1944 was a shadow of its former self. Four years of combat losses, including millions of dead on the Eastern Front, had created a huge manpower problem for Hitler, particularly as the Allied forces closed in on Germany.

FINDING THE SOLDIERS

To boost manpower, Germany's replacement, training, and rear-echelon formations were combed from top to bottom to find men who could be diverted to frontline service. The results were often not promising. A young man whose principal experience had been refueling aircraft or administering supplies could find himself suddenly thrust into bitter fighting on the Eastern Front. So the late-war German unit often became a mix of dwindling numbers of veterans attempting

to organize new recruits into some semblance of a professional force.

Another ingredient of the late-war German defense was the *Volkssturm* (People's Army). Largely an act of desperation, the *Volkssturm* was formed in October 1944 and drew all males between 16 and 60 into military service,

▲ Allied troops march past the ruins of Monte Cassino, Italy, in May 1944. It cost the Allies 50,000 casualties to capture the town and the nearby mountain and monastery.

◄ A bare-chested GI takes a shave in snow-covered surroundings during a lull in the Battle of the Bulge, Ardennes Forest, 1945. Cases of frostbite became common among the U.S. troops when lighting a fire was often not an option—the flames and smoke would attract enemy artillery fire.

WAFFEN-SS TROOPER, 1944

The Waffen-SS was the combat arm of Heinrich Himmler's SS. Although at the beginning of the war it prided itself on its "pure German" ancestry, by 1944 it was heavily manned by foreign troops, mainly from Eastern Europe.

Webbing
The leather straps here support a belt, on which are canvas MP44 ammunition pouches.

MP44
The MP44 was history's first issue assault rifle, a full auto weapon firing an "intermediate" 7.92-mm round.

Camouflage
The oakleaf pattern camouflage was reversible, with color options for both spring/ summer and fall.

if they weren't already. So, in those last dreadful months of the war, the Allies encountered both young boys and old men in action. The boys in particular could be fanatical fighters, having been imbued with the ideology of the Hitler Youth.

DEFEAT AND OCCUPATION

Although by 1944 it was clear that Germany was heading for defeat, there were still no easy victories for the Allies. Battles in northern Italy, the Ardennes Forest and Berlin proved that the German discipline and tactical commitment remained, despite the manpower issues. Many Allied troops not at the front line, however, began the experience of occupying the territory of the enemy. Relations between Germans and occupiers could at times be amicable, as both sides began to rebuild devastated territory. Yet there were problems. Indiscipline owing to drink and the impending end of service became rife among soldiers. Far more seriously, on the Eastern Front many Soviet soldiers indulged in systematic rape—an estimated 1.5 million German women were brutalized this way in 1944–45.

▼ Chief of the SS Heinrich Himmler (background, center) observes the march-past of newly formed *Volkssturm* units in Berlin, November 1944. The men are armed with Panzerfaust antitank weapons.

U.S. "ISLAND HOPPING"

Island hopping is a pleasant-sounding term for what was in reality a truly dreadful experience. For three years, the United States forces fought across the Pacific, losing tens of thousands of men on scraps of land most had never heard of before.

America's "island-hopping" campaign ran from 1943 to 1945 in the Central Pacific theater. It was an unforgiving action, as Japanese defenders held on to small and seemingly insignificant tropical atolls and islands with suicidal commitment, determined to stop U.S. forces reaching the Japanese homeland. Places such as Tarawa, Saipan, Peleliu, Iwo Jima, and Okinawa became infamous because of the ferocity of the fighting there. To gain an insight into the soldier's experience of island hopping, the battle of Iwo Jima offers a salutary case study.

> "It takes **courage** to stay at the front on Iwo Jima ...to push out **against an unseen enemy**."
>
> U.S. MARINE VETERAN

LETTER HOME

"Hello Darling, I'm writing on the edge of my foxhole as I write this, the guns are pounding away and to top it off I can't think of a darned thing to say. Pardon me while I light my pipe. Betsy I feel like a heel. You've been so swell about writing and I've been so negligent. I haven't any excuse for not writing that's what baffles me. Every time I get a blank piece of paper in front of me my mind gets just as blank."
—A U.S. Marine on Iwo Jima

IWO JIMA

Some 70,000 American troops (mainly U.S. Marines) were committed to the battle of Iwo Jima (February 19–March 26, 1945). What was astonishing was the level of casualties experienced on a piece of terrain that measured just 8 sq miles/21 km² in size. In five weeks of fighting, the Marines lost 26,038 dead and wounded; of the 21,000 Japanese defenders, 18,844 were killed, and just 216 taken prisoner.

◄ American soldiers take a break during a lull in the fighting on Iwo Jima. During the five-week battle, half of the Marines would be either killed or wounded in action.

Before the first U.S. boats landed on Iwo Jima, the Japanese had turned the volcanic island into a fortress. The Japanese took the plentiful volcanic ash and mixed it with concrete to build hundreds of shell-resistant strongpoints. In total they dug 11 miles/18 km of interconnected caves and tunnels into the rocky landscape, with narrow openings nearly impossible to spot from the outside.

SLUGGING IT OUT

On stepping ashore the U.S. soldiers sank up to their calves in the crumbling volcanic surface. Amtrac amphibious vehicles were unable to gain traction, becoming immobile targets. In just that first day of fighting, 2,420 Americans were killed.

The U.S. forces eventually consolidated the beachhead and took the island. But every single strongpoint, cave, tunnel, outcrop, and bunker had to be cleared by small teams, often at high cost, while American firepower dealt with suicidal *banzai* charges. In one charge, for example, on March 8, up to 800 Japanese troops were mown down by American fire. The U.S. combat units on Iwo Jima took around 50 percent casualties. Twenty-six men were awarded the Medal of Honor.

▲ This U.S. Army webbing system consisted of a belt strung with M1 Garand rifle clip pouches, plus a water bottle, first-aid kit, entrenching tool, small backpack, and a bayonet frog.

U.S. ARMY SERGEANT, PACIFIC 1945
Generally speaking, the U.S. Army invested less in camouflage uniforms than the Marine Corps. A two-piece herringbone twill outfit was issued from 1943, for use in both Europe and the Pacific.

Grenade
The Mk II fragmentation grenade was an essential tool for clearing bunkers. It had a five-second fuse delay.

M1A1 Thompson
This submachine gun had a 500-rpm rate of fire.

Camouflage
As the pant turnups indicate, the Army camouflage fabric was reversible, with brown colors dominant on one side and green on the other.

> "Fight no battle **unprepared**, fight no battle you are not **sure of winning**; make every effort to prepare for each battle, make every effort to **ensure victory**..."
>
> MAO TSE-TUNG, CHINESE COMMUNIST LEADER

THE MODERN ERA

At every level, the art of soldiering has been revolutionized since the end of World War II, with technology being the primary instigator of change. Compared to soldiers of 100 years before, the kit, uniforms, equipment, and weaponry of the modern soldier is the stuff of science fiction. Yet the basic needs of the soldier remain largely the same.

◀ Soldiers from the U.S. 101st Airborne Division make a deployment from a CH-47 Chinook helicopter in eastern Afghanistan, 2002. One of the seminal developments in land forces warfare since 1945 has been the advent and growth of helicopter battlefield mobility.

NEW WORLD ORDER

Two key factors have transformed the life of the soldier since 1945. The first is technological, with seminal advances in military materiél and computerized weaponry. The second is social—since 1945, the life of the soldier has been revealed by the media in unprecedented detail.

Although the global catastrophe that was World War II ended in 1945, the world was unable to experience even a day of peace. A World War gave way to the Cold War, a clash between Soviet Communism and Western capitalism fought in dozens of major and minor proxy wars around the planet. Added to this picture were the many postcolonial conflicts, the clash between Arab nations and Israel, and the rise of international terrorism. Even when the Cold War ended in 1989, the fractured world did not find peace. The international community fought a major war in the Middle East in 1990–91 following the Iraqi invasion of Kuwait, and lengthy conflicts in Iraq and Afghanistan were triggered by the terrorist attacks on the United States in 2001. The more recent "Arab Spring" uprisings, plus the horrific campaigns of the Islamic State (IS) in Syria and Iraq, means that conflict remains a priority news item.

TECHNOLOGY

Within this context, every aspect of the soldier's life—communications, weaponry, uniform, personal kit, logistics and transport, nutrition, and much more—has been the beneficiary of the huge leaps made in science and computerization from the 1950s onward. A U.S. infantry soldier in 1945, for example, had an eight-shot

> "Desert Storm left **one awful legacy**: It imposed the idea that you must be able to **fight the wars** of the future **without suffering losses.**"
>
> GENERAL PHILIPPE MORILLON

◀ French troops disembark in Algiers harbor during the Algerian War (1954–62). The conflict was one of many postcolonial wars around the world at this time.

PHOTO POWER

Photojournalism was critical in shaping public opinion of the Vietnam War between 1953 and 1975. Key photographic moments included Nick Ut's image of a naked, injured girl running hysterically from a napalm strike in 1972 and Eddie Adams' photo of the execution of a Viet Cong suspect in Saigon in 1968. Such images tapped directly into the mood of the antiwar movement.

semiauto Garand rifle and wore a basic
olive-drab uniform, fabric webbing
system, and an M1 steel helmet. Today's
equivalent, by contrast, has a selective-
fire assault rifle, a ballistic, advanced
combat helmet fitted with integrated
comms and head-cam, a sophisticated
and comfortable camouflage uniform
designed to reduce the soldier's visual
signature to infrared (IR) and night-
vision devices, and an ergonomically
contoured load-bearing system.

MEDIA COVERAGE
Since 1945, media access has also
been reshaped by technology, with the
advent and growth of broadcast news,
embedded reporters traveling with units
of troops, and the internet. Soldiers'
actions have consequently become far

▲ An Israeli self-propelled howitzer
pounds enemy positions in the
Syrian desert during the 1973 Yom
Kippur War. The IDF is one of the
world's most combat-experienced
armed forces.

more visible, the realities of military
life and actual combat exposed for the
world to see. The soldier has therefore
come under pressure to justify
individual actions previously hidden in
the fog of war.

▶ Some aspects of soldiering remain unchanged, such
as exhausting route marches in full pack.

KOREA 1950–53

Although U.S. forces made up the bulk of the United Nations army deployed to Korea in 1950, the conflict drew in men and women from more than 15 nations, as diverse as the United Kingdom, Australia, France, the Netherlands, South Africa, and Thailand.

The Korean War was the first Cold War conflict, triggered when United States-backed South Korea was invaded by communist North Korea on June 25, 1950. The West responded by sending a huge army under the umbrella of the United Nations (UN), and found itself fighting not only the North Vietnamese, but also the Chinese Army, which entered the conflict in October 1950. Fought for three bitter years, the war eventually reached stalemate virtually where it began, on the 38th parallel.

UN SOLDIERS

American forces were the core of the UN Army, but at first most of the troops deployed to Korea were those on occupation duties in Japan. Many were undertrained, unfit, and had poor equipment; troops with combat experience composed only about 15 percent of the ranks. These soldiers, thrown against a highly motivated

▲ A group of American soldiers sit in a ditch at the side of a road in Korea. Although regular troops were used at first, by the time the war ended more than 220,000 Americans had been drafted into the conflict.

communist army, suffered a series of disastrous retreats and defeats, until the UN ranks were fleshed out and strengthened in the fall.

The first experience of Korea for most UN soldiers was of an almost medieval world. Fighting in and around isolated and obscure villages with names that to Western tongues were almost unpronounceable, winter or mountainous operations exposed the troops to temperatures of -4°F/-20°C, while in summer temperatures reached

EYEWITNESS ACCOUNT

"We left in pouring rain, which blew in through the open sides of the jeep. The going was slow. The unsurfaced road was rough, slippery, and jammed with retreating South Koreans who paid no heed to time or weather. Trucks, traveling without headlights, roared along as fast as they dared. Before dawn, we passed at least half a dozen that had toppled down the steep levees into the flooded rice fields below."

—Journalist Dennis Warner, on his way to the front line, Korea, 1950

▲ The 1937-pattern webbing equipment shown here was still in use by British forces during the Korean War, as were many of the weapons used in World War II—the Lee-Enfield No.4 and Bren Gun.

near-tropical levels. The combat experience could also be intense, with some clashes as fierce as those of World War II.

COMMUNIST SOLDIERS

The forces arrayed against the UN and South Koreans were heavy on manpower, but lacking in leadership and equipment. They frequently suffered logistical breakdowns, on account of U.S. bombing raids, hence food, ammunition, and clothing could be in short supply. Frostbite and hypothermia were common in winter, and casualties were appalling owing to crude frontal-attack tactics.

▼ North Korean and Chinese troops celebrate a victory. The communist soldiers were heavily indoctrinated with Maoist theories of warfare.

U.S. INFANTRYMAN, KOREA, 1950

This soldier's olive-drab herringbone twill combat uniform is protected by a 1950-pattern rain poncho; this item was essentially the World War II poncho, but with a hood added for extra protection. The M1 helmet is still the standard headgear.

Poncho
The rain poncho was made of nylon twill and coated with vinyl resin.

M1 Garand
The standard U.S. rifle was still the semiauto M1 Garand, which had a range of around 650 yards/600 m.

M1943 Boot
The soldier wears the World War II-era M1943 double-buckle boot.

REVOLUTIONARY ARMIES

Revolutionary armies subverted the concepts of how to wage war. Individually, the soldiers were often poorly equipped and trained compared to modern Western forces, but they compensated through intelligent group tactics and personal tenacity.

Communist ideology was central to the life of the revolutionary soldier. Discipline of thought and deed was rigorously monitored by political officers to guard against "corruption" by outside influences. In the Viet Cong (the communist insurgents operating within South Vietnam during the 1950s–70s), for example, the units were divided into three-man groups, each man responsible for monitoring the others for lapses in ideological purity. Daily "self-criticism" sessions were held, in which each person confessed to their personal failings. The important point

▲ The AK-47 is history's most mass-produced firearm. It was adopted as the standard Soviet rifle in 1948.

▼ Fidel Castro, leader of Cuba's revolutionary forces, with members of his staff, at a secret base in 1957. Revolutionary soldiers often direct their loyalty toward a single inspirational leader, rather than a political idea.

"A revolution is a **struggle to the death** between the **future** and the **past.**"

FIDEL CASTRO

was that the soldier showed complete loyalty to both the political ideology and to his leaders. He was encouraged to look upon his unit commander as a "father" and political officer as a "mother," placing these relationships above all others.

GROUP ACTION
One defining characteristic of the revolutionary armies is their application of mass manpower to achieve their objectives. This was in part born of necessity. Although the socialist vision was based on everyone having all their material needs fulfilled, the field insurgents tended to be short of food, equipment, vehicles, and weapons. Because of this, militarized human labor became the chief means of overcoming obstacles and hardships. In post-revolutionary Cuba in 1973, Fidel Castro established the Ejército Juvenil del Trabajo (EJT; Youth Labor Army). Trained in the basic tactics of warfare for civil defense, the young men and women in the EJT were put to work on farms or on construction and railroad projects.

LIFE IN THE FIELD
During times of conflict, the life of the revolutionary soldier tended to be unremittingly hard and spartan.

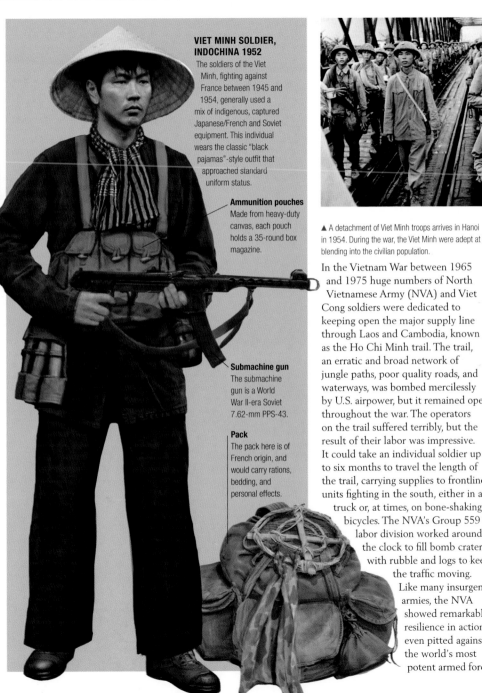

VIET MINH SOLDIER, INDOCHINA 1952

The soldiers of the Viet Minh, fighting against France between 1945 and 1954, generally used a mix of indigenous, captured Japanese/French and Soviet equipment. This individual wears the classic "black pajamas"-style outfit that approached standard uniform status.

Ammunition pouches
Made from heavy-duty canvas, each pouch holds a 35-round box magazine.

Submachine gun
The submachine gun is a World War II-era Soviet 7.62-mm PPS-43.

Pack
The pack here is of French origin, and would carry rations, bedding, and personal effects.

▲ A detachment of Viet Minh troops arrives in Hanoi in 1954. During the war, the Viet Minh were adept at blending into the civilian population.

In the Vietnam War between 1965 and 1975 huge numbers of North Vietnamese Army (NVA) and Viet Cong soldiers were dedicated to keeping open the major supply line through Laos and Cambodia, known as the Ho Chi Minh trail. The trail, an erratic and broad network of jungle paths, poor quality roads, and waterways, was bombed mercilessly by U.S. airpower, but it remained open throughout the war. The operators on the trail suffered terribly, but the result of their labor was impressive. It could take an individual soldier up to six months to travel the length of the trail, carrying supplies to frontline units fighting in the south, either in a truck or, at times, on bone-shaking bicycles. The NVA's Group 559 labor division worked around the clock to fill bomb craters with rubble and logs to keep the traffic moving. Like many insurgency armies, the NVA showed remarkable resilience in action, even pitted against the world's most potent armed forces.

THE VIETNAM EXPERIENCE 1965–75

The Vietnam War remains a period of trauma in the American psyche. Millions served in the war, and more than 58,000 lost their lives "in country." The nature of the conflict also placed a profound strain on the young soldiers' minds and bodies.

It is difficult to generalize on the experience of the soldier in Vietnam, because it depended hugely upon the individual's role. Soldiering in Vietnam ranged from managing logistics at a support base in Da Nang through to top-secret special forces raids into Laos and Cambodia. But for tens of thousands of American infantry and Marines on or around the front lines in South Vietnam, there was a grim pattern to much of daily life.

DEPLOYMENT

Most U.S. soldiers were 17–25 years old, drafted or volunteered, and sent to Vietnam for a fixed 12–13-month period of service, with a known exit date (the DEROS—Date of Expected Return from Overseas). This system has now been recognized as problematic for morale. Although it meant that the soldier knew when he would leave, it also meant that the DEROS became an obsessive focus, demoralizing the soldier at the start, and making him fear for his survival toward the end.

There were large-scale battles in the Vietnam War, such as those that occurred during the Tet Offensive in 1968, but many of the operations consisted of relatively small but

▲ Staving off heat exhaustion, U.S. troops of the 25th Infantry Division rehydrate during a patrol through South Vietnam's jungles and paddy fields in 1967.

AK-47
With its reliability and heavy firepower, the AK-47 was the standard NVA weapon and a clear sign of Soviet/ Chinese support.

Chi-Com pouches
The "Chi-Com" (Chinese communist) chest pouches were ideal for AK-47 magazines.

Sandals
Simple sandals were cut from automobile tires or other sources of rubber, creating cheap but durable footwear.

NORTH VIETNAMESE ARMY SOLDIER, 1965
While the Viet Cong tended to dress in regular civilian clothing, the North Vietnamese Army (NVA) had a formal, albeit simple, uniform, subject to variations based on source. Soviet, Chinese, local, and aging colonial items were also put to use.

> "This is not a jungle war, but a **struggle for freedom** on every front of **human activity.**"
>
> U.S. PRESIDENT LYNDON B JOHNSON

aggressive U.S. patrols of defined rural areas. Heavily laden with ammunition and kit, American soldiers would spend hours sweating in the tropical humidity. Casualties most commonly came from low-level ambushes or booby traps, with the enemy often not seen. The steady and traumatic losses, and the fact that in some areas U.S. soldiers might experience combat every single day, produced enormous psychological tension. Recent research has found that about 31 percent of Vietnam veterans suffered from post-traumatic stress disorder (PTSD).

UNPOPULAR WAR

The Vietnam experience was made more demoralizing for U.S. soldiers because the conflict largely lost the support of the American public. Thus when the soldiers returned home, the reception could be cold, even hostile.

▼ U.S. "air cavalry" move to board a UH-1 helicopter prior to an operation in 1968. Helicopters were the primary means of in-theater transportation.

U.S. MARINE, VIETNAM, 1968
Even on light patrol operations, U.S. soldiers took much more kit into the field than the comparable NVA soldier. This Marine wears a heavy M1952 flak jacket over his basic jungle uniform, to protect against small-arms fire and shell splinters.

Bandolier
The chest bandolier contains additional magazines for the M16 rifle.

M16A1
The 5.56-mm M16A1 was the replacement for the 7.62-mm M14.

Jungle boot
The combination leather and canvas boot featured ventilation and drainage holes on the outer side.

ARAB AND ISRAELI FORCES 1948–73

From the very establishment of the State of Israel, in 1948, the Israel Defense Forces (IDF) were fighting for the country's existence. Against them were a broad spectrum of Arab armies, many of them sponsored by the military expertise of foreign powers.

The IDF was created by order of Israel's Defense Minister, David Ben Gurion, on May 26, 1948. It was a conscript force, put together at speed to face the threat of surrounding Arab enemies— the combined forces of six armies had attacked the fledgling state on May 15.

▶ Israeli troops in armored vehicles advance against what were far less well-equipped Egyptian troops at the start of the Six-Day War, June 5, 1967, near Rafah, Gaza Strip.

VETERANS

The men who made up the early ranks of the IDF were a thoroughly mixed bunch. Some were recent immigrants to the country, many of them World War II veterans from Eastern Europe. Indigenous combat experience came from the ranks of men from the Irgun, Haganah, and Lehi underground organizations, which had fought against the British and Arabs during the 1930s and 40s. So, while many within the

> "The air was full of the **smell of cordite** and the smoke of **burning tanks on the ridge.**"
>
> AVIGDOR KAHALANI, IDF
> VETERAN, YOM KIPPUR WAR

Israeli ranks were raw recruits, a very large number were combat-experienced veterans, a fact that served the IDF well during its first decade.

In its early days, IDF soldiers had to cope with an unhelpfully diverse range of equipment. There was almost no standardization of weaponry or uniforms, for example. By the mid-1950s, however, the IDF soldiers were

THE UZI

One of the defining weapons of the IDF soldier from 1951 until the 1970s was the Uzi submachine gun. Developed by IDF officer Uziel Gal, and based on Czech designs, it could fire 9-mm bullets at 900 rpm, with an effective range of about 180 yards/200 m. It was also highly reliable in dusty conditions.

◀ Israeli soldiers on patrol during the Six-Day War, 1967. Most are armed with early variants of the Belgian 7.62-mm FN FAL rifle, one of the world's most widely used guns.

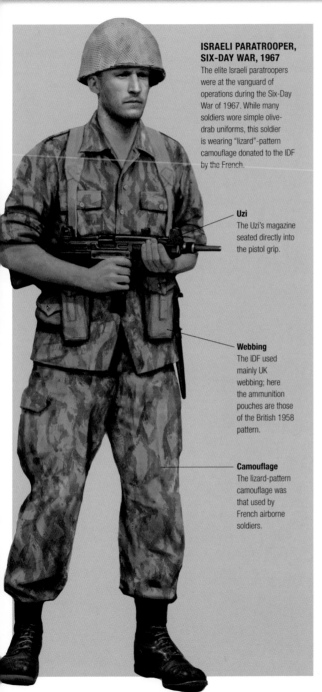

ISRAELI PARATROOPER, SIX-DAY WAR, 1967

The elite Israeli paratroopers were at the vanguard of operations during the Six-Day War of 1967. While many soldiers wore simple olive-drab uniforms, this soldier is wearing "lizard"-pattern camouflage donated to the IDF by the French.

Uzi
The Uzi's magazine seated directly into the pistol grip.

Webbing
The IDF used mainly UK webbing; here the ammunition pouches are those of the British 1958 pattern.

Camouflage
The lizard-pattern camouflage was that used by French airborne soldiers.

professionalizing, and by the two major wars of 1967 and 1973 they boasted some of the best-trained and most combat-experienced troops in the world—reservists and regular soldiers alike—hence their repeated victories.

ARAB ARMIES

The Arab forces were sizable and had powerful resources, but the individual soldier was often under-equipped, poorly trained, and badly led. The most professional of the soldiers were to be found in Iraq, Jordan, and Egypt, all of which had strong historical military connections with Britain. Nevertheless, the lack of tactical cohesion and logistics had terrible consequences for the Arab fighters. During the 1967 Six-Day War, an estimated 20,000 Egyptian soldiers died of heatstroke in the Sinai Desert, their limited water rations not being sufficient for the exertions of combat or the heat of the desert.

▼ Israeli soldiers eat a meal in the shadow of their armored vehicle. Egyptian soldiers weren't so fortunate, and suffered from poor supplies of food and water.

RUSSIAN NIGHTMARES

Russia fought two disastrous wars during the 1980s and 1990s, the first in Afghanistan in the Soviet era (1979–89) and another in Chechnya (1994–96), after the fall of the Berlin Wall. Both conflicts exposed the brutal life of the average Russian conscript.

If we take a snapshot of the Soviet Army in 1985, when the war in Afghanistan was at its height, we see the product of a militarized society. Every year about 75 percent of eligible 18-year-olds were drafted for service into the armed forces, receiving just four weeks of basic training before being sent to their units. Once in garrison, the new soldiers were completely subjugated to the violent whim of the NCOs. Physical bullying was, and remains, a terrible problem in Russian forces, part of the process of *dedovshchina*—literally "grandfatherism," but more akin to "initiation." A report by *The New York Times* in 2006 found that in one year 292 young soldiers were killed under this process. Combined with almost no leave and stark barrack conditions, suicide and injury were common.

▼ Russian soldiers are deployed by helicopter to Grozny, Chechnya, after its capture by Russian forces.

AFGHANISTAN

The Soviet forces entered Afghanistan in 1979, attempting to prop up a Soviet-leaning government against a powerful Islamic insurgency. Despite their superior weapons and resources,

▲ Afghan *mujahideen* leader Amin Wardak, surrounded by his combatants. Note the eclectic mix of weapons and the absence of modern military kit.

EYEWITNESS ACCOUNT

"You get a beating for anything at all. If a spirit doesn't show respect in his conversation with an older soldier, a 'Grandad,' he'll get beaten up. If he lies on his bed in the day, he'll get beaten up. If the people back home send him good rubber slippers and he decides to wear them in the shower, he'll get beaten up and lose his slippers."
—Arkady Babchenko, veteran of the First Chechen War, in *One Soldier's War in Chechnya* (Portobello, 2007)

> "I didn't really want [to serve] because we knew there was a **war going on** and the **probability of dying** was very high."
>
> TINIBEK KADIROV, RUSSIAN WAR VETERAN

the Soviet units lost men steadily to the *mujahideen* enemy, who knew the terrain far better than their opponents. Insanitary conditions also inflicted heavy losses—nearly 14,500 men were killed in action, 53,700 wounded, and 416,000 suffered from serious illness, such as hepatitis, dysentery, and typhoid. The Soviets withdrew from Afghanistan in 1989, but by this time possibly more than a million Afghan civilians had been killed.

CHECHNYA

One of the first major postcommunist wars for Russia, that in Chechnya in 1994–96, was no more successful. Morale virtually collapsed within the armed forces, by virtue of constant fighting and casualties, the endemic bullying, and also problems in paying soldiers after the collapse of the Soviet Union. Illegal drug use among the Russian troops became worryingly high. Indeed, some witnesses in Grozny around 1996 claim that it was not unheard of for terrified young soldiers to sell their weapons to rebel forces for narcotics, only to be killed by those same guns during a subsequent assault. It was understood that being captured by the Chechen guerrillas meant almost certain death.

The war in Chechnya ended with a forced peace treaty in 1996, although the Russians would fight another brutal war there between 1990 and 2000.

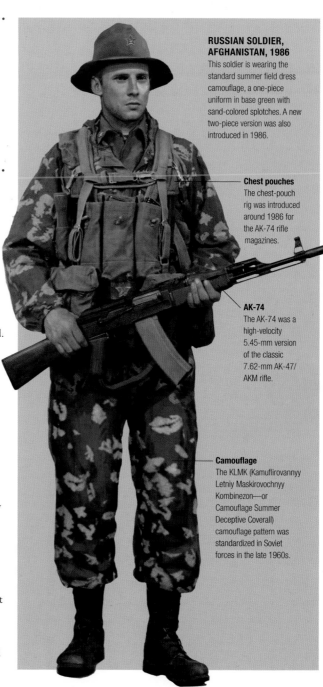

RUSSIAN SOLDIER, AFGHANISTAN, 1986
This soldier is wearing the standard summer field dress camouflage, a one-piece uniform in base green with sand-colored splotches. A new two-piece version was also introduced in 1986.

Chest pouches
The chest-pouch rig was introduced around 1986 for the AK-74 rifle magazines.

AK-74
The AK-74 was a high-velocity 5.45-mm version of the classic 7.62-mm AK-47/ AKM rifle.

Camouflage
The KLMK (Kamuflirovannyy Letniy Maskirovochnyy Kombinezon—or Camouflage Summer Deceptive Coverall) camouflage pattern was standardized in Soviet forces in the late 1960s.

WAR ON TERROR, AFGHANISTAN

The war in Afghanistan against the Taliban, which began in October 2001, has been the longest-running conflict in American history. Hundreds of thousands of soldiers, of various nationalities, have now served tours of duty in the war-torn nation.

Most soldiers of the International Security and Assistance Force (ISAF) coalition in Afghanistan would be based in one of the huge camps, forward operating bases (FOBs), or main operating bases (MOBs) dotted at strategic locations around the country. Some of these were on an epic scale, acting as hubs for logistics, aviation, mechanized ops, and troop movements.

▶ Col. William Huff of the U.S. Army's 82nd Airborne Division sits and talks with local Afghan leaders. Gaining the trust of the local communities has been a key ingredient of the ISAF operations in Afghanistan.

▼ British soldiers from the Bomb Squad, Helmand Task Force, dispose of unexploded ordnance, in this case mortar bombs.

CAMP BASTION

Life for soldiers within these hubs was a far cry from rough combat outposts. Camp Bastion, for example, was a huge logistics airbase, covering an area of about 10 sq miles/26 km^2 and home to up to 30,000 people at any one time. It was primarily used by British forces plus troops of the Afghan National Army (ANA) and U.S. Marines.

Most of the troops deployed to Bastion would sleep in high-quality tented accommodation, the largest tents sleeping up to 32 people. Work spaces were frequently air conditioned, essential in a country of seasonal weather extremes. Entertainment was limited on the base, although a Pizza Hut, bars, and several gymnasiums, plus various improvised and formal sports, provided recreation. The impressive ISAF logistics also meant that food was in plentiful supply—around 27 tons of salad and fruit were flown into the base each month. To maintain morale, the soldiers also enjoyed direct communications with home via internet

U.S. SPECIAL OPS SOLDIER, AFGHANISTAN

U.S. Special Forces often display more personal choice in uniform, weaponry, and kit than regular army soldiers. They will even augment their military items with civilian or foreign military kit at their own expense, if they think the kit provides a tactical enhancement.

Comms
This soldier has a chest-mounted comms system, plus headphones.

M4 Carbine
The standard M4 carbine has been heavily customized with optical sight, IR illuminator, and tactical light.

Helmet
The Special Ops Ballistic helmet comes with integral NVG mount.

Knee protectors
Thick pads protect the knees when the soldier is crawling or shooting from a kneeling position.

> "I could **hear rounds** cracking over my head. The **adrenaline started pumping** right away."
>
> MARINE CORPS PFC. TIMOTHY WORKMAN

and phone, while more than 70,000 pallets of mail were delivered to the base each month, providing a weekly morale boost.

ON OPS

Outside the major bases, life was very different. Offensives and patrols frequently brought contact with the Taliban, producing vicious firefights, sometimes of days' duration. Improvised explosive devices (IEDs) were a constant threat, tackled by explosive ordnance disposal (EOD) officers with weary regularity. In terms of the enemy, the division between civilian and combatant was blurred, adding to the confusion. Some U.S. studies have revealed that an estimated 10–18 percent of veterans have PTSD.

▼ The internet has transformed military communications. Here U.S. soldiers at Camp Bastion, Afghanistan, make internet voice calls home or catch up on e-mails.

FACETS OF WAR: FEMALE SOLDIERS

For most of history, women have either been absent from the battlefield or have served in support roles, with some rare exceptions. In the last 70 years, however, the status of women in the military has been transformed.

Female warriors have long captured the public imagination, but for complex social, physical, and psychological reasons, women have traditionally been thought unsuited to the dire business of military killing, despite the evidence that periodically arises to the contrary. Those women who stepped outside convention and embraced the military way of life therefore became iconic figures in history. Names such as Artemisia of Caria (5th century BC), Boudicca (1st century AD), Joan of Arc (15th century), and Hannah Snell (18th century) ring out from school history books surrounded by as much mythology as fact, simultaneously proving women's capacity for martial service and displaying its rarity.

SUPPORT SERVICES
Setting aside the legendary figures of female militarism, the fact remains that women have always been essential

▲ Hannah Snell (1723–92) was a British woman who disguised herself as a man to enter military service. She distinguished herself in combat and was awarded a military pension on her eventual discharge.

▼ Soldiers of a Russian women's battalion. Many of the female units were given the title "Battalion of Death," to indicate their ferocity and commitment.

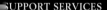

TIMELINE

1917 The Russian revolutionary government authorizes the formation of exclusively female combat units; a total of 6,000 women serve in these units.

1917–18 In support roles, 21,480 nurses serve in the U.S. military during the last two years of the war.

1940–44 Women of the British Auxiliary Territorial Service take responsibilities for operating antiaircraft guns against German bombing raids.

1941–45 The Red Army fields numerous female snipers, some of whom have astonishing kill records numbering in the hundreds.

1963–1975 During the Vietnam War, women serve as active combatants in both the NVA and the Viet Cong.

1973 From the Yom Kippur War, women start to serve in more combat and training roles within the IDF (previously they had mainly been deployed in administration and education).

1991 Congress authorizes women to fly as combat pilots in the U.S. Air Force.

2005 Sergeant Leigh Ann Hester becomes the first American woman to be awarded the Silver Star.

2014 The UK Defense Secretary announces that women will be trained to serve in all frontline combat roles in the British Army.

adjuncts to the business of war. From ancient times until the 20th century, women were often found working as camp followers, performing a wide range of menial but essential support services for the fighting men. Their role as battlefield nurses was also set during the 18th and 19th centuries, a duty that took the women right up to the front lines at times.

COMBAT SERVICE

Women continued to perform support duties in the 20th century, but we also see a progressive widening of their responsibilities up to and including that of combatant. This shift was partly practical—during the emergencies of the World Wars, some nations resorted to female soldiers to help plug manpower shortages. From the 1960s onward, the changes were also partly fueled by the growth of the women's rights movement. During World War II women were found, especially in the Soviet Union, in frontline roles such as

▲ Female *peshmergas* (fighters) have fought alongside their Kurdish menfolk against the IS insurgents in Iraq.

▼ A female U.S. Army soldier in Afghanistan, 2003. Female troops have been culturally invaluable for interacting with Afghan women.

combat pilot, antiaircraft gunner, and sniper. In the postwar world, North Vietnam, Israel, and North Korea centrally integrated women into their military structures. Today in most European and American armies, there are few specific roles that women are barred from performing.

WAR ON TERROR, IRAQ

The war in Iraq began with a U.S.-led invasion in 2003. Although the offensive was a rapid success, few Western leaders had foreseen the prolonged insurgency that resulted, costing the lives of thousands of troops and tens of thousands of civilians.

Some of the key characteristics of living and operating in Iraq were dictated by the terrain. Iraq is extremely flat, hot, and dry almost all year round. Dust storms could bring entire columns of troops to a halt for days. The Middle Eastern sun constantly threatened heat exhaustion, so regular "hydration stops" were scheduled to keep body fluid levels high. In the early stages of the invasion in 2003, it was believed that Saddam Hussein's forces would use chemical weapons, so soldiers drilled frequently in putting on their

Mission Oriented Protective Posture (MOPP) suits, which were positively suffocating in the heat.

TRAUMA

The war in Iraq was hugely traumatic for the many thousands of coalition troops deployed. Fighting often took place within densely populated urban areas, with the result that civilian casualties were witnessed at graphic close quarters. One major research project into the experience of U.S. soldiers in Iraq placed shock at the scale and horrific nature

> "The **only thing**
> I supported
> was the
> **commitment**
> I had made
> to **my fellow
> soldiers.**"
>
> U.S. ARMY OFFICER

RPG-7
The RPG-7 is the world's most prolific shoulder-launched antiarmor weapon.

Black outfit
The black outfit of the *Fedayeen* might be accented by a checkered scarf.

Combat boots
This fighter wears a pair of regular army leather boots.

IRAQI *FEDAYEEN* FIGHTER, 2003
The *Fedayeen Saddam* were a paramilitary group who fought against the NATO forces during and beyond the invasion of Iraq in 2003. It was a volunteer army, and hence did not have standard-issue uniform or kit. However, the black outfit here was common, and they relied heavily on RPGs (as shown here), AK rifles, IEDs, and crude mortars.

▲ A soldier of the Explosive Ordnance Disposal Special Unit studies an area in which an IED has been emplaced. He checks for warning signs, such as individuals who might remotely detonate the explosive device.

▶ U.S. soldiers speak to an Iraqi child accompanying her mother (not seen) to attend a ceremony marking the end of a two-month training course run by the U.S. military in west Baghdad in 2009.

▼ U.S. Marines use a phone center to call friends and relatives from Camp Fallujah. Such calls had some risks: any bad news from home could affect a soldier's morale.

of the violence at the top of the list of emotional impressions. IEDs were also a constant and grinding threat. One Iraq veteran, Mark Lanchance, described the psychological effect of IEDs: "Imagine this...next time you are driving down the road and you are going to work or home, look at every guard rail, every trash can, every cement kerb, and all those things could blow up at any moment. Just think about that. Everything that is there is prospectively your enemy." Some statistics from Iraq, compiled by the U.S. National Center for PTSD, show that in Iraq 95 percent of American soldiers said that they had seen dead bodies, 93 percent had been shot at, 89 percent had been ambushed or attacked, and 86 percent personally knew someone who had been killed or wounded. The same statistics for Afghanistan are 50 percent or less.

KEEPING IN TOUCH

A critical morale booster for a soldier is keeping in touch with loved ones at home. Calling home could be done via commercial payphones, military-provided VOIP phones, webcams, and cell phones. In addition to that support network, most armies in Iraq were professional units, which meant that there was strong group cohesion.

THE COMPUTERIZATION OF WAR

Today's soldier is the beneficiary of incredible advances in technology, particularly in communications, surveillance, and weaponry. Getting the technological balance right, however, is complicated, as too much advanced kit can hamper rather than enhance soldiering.

It is important to remember that many military forces around the world, especially those in developing regions, are still working with levels of kit and technology not dissimilar to those carried by soldiers in World War II. An olive-drab uniform, AK rifle, clutch of grenades, VHF radio, and some basic mortar or artillery support is the technological extent for millions of soldiers. Yet for those men and women fortunate enough to serve in the most advanced armies, the technological picture is strikingly different.

THE SMARTPHONE BATTLEFIELD

One bit of non-standard kit carried by almost all soldiers today is a smartphone. From the moment cell phones became portable enough to carry in a pocket, in the 1990s, these devices proved invaluable to soldiers, if only for keeping in touch with

family or, when main comms had failed, reconnecting with other units and individuals. Today's smartphones have far greater tactical potential. For example, the United States' Defense Advanced Research Projects Agency (DARPA) is currently developing militarized smartphone apps that

▲ Today's military headquarters are major communication hubs, gathering and processing information from dozens of data sources across the battlespace.

THE NETWORKED BATTLESPACE

Today's professional military forces aspire to a fully networked battlespace. In this arena, all army, navy, and air force units and systems are connected through a secure communications network, fluidly and instantly sharing surveillance and combat information in real time to give forces a huge tactical advantage over less advanced enemies. The diagram here shows how assets can be connected, but the routes of communication can shift according to tactical requirements.

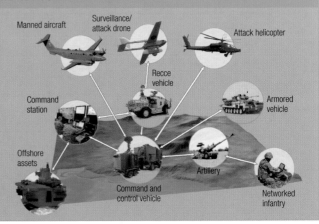

Manned aircraft

Surveillance/ attack drone

Attack helicopter

Recce vehicle

Command station

Armored vehicle

Offshore assets

Artillery

Command and control vehicle

Networked infantry

can deliver vital real-time battlefield information straight to the soldier's handset. The handsets will be fitted with "ruggedized" covers and a week's worth of power will be supplied by a back-mounted battery pack. Interestingly, in the U.K. researchers are developing uniforms that actually collect the static generated by the moving fabric to charge up such electrical devices.

WEAPONS AND SUPPORT

Advanced smartphone apps are just the tip of the technological iceberg. A soldier's ability to conduct surveillance and reconnaissance was reshaped by the advent of unmanned aerial vehicles (UAVs), or drones. Fitted with high-resolution daytime- and thermal-imaging cameras, the drones are either piloted by in-field soldiers or by pilots many miles away (even in different countries), beaming the collected imagery straight to command station computers or battlefield monitors. Using laser- and GPS-designation

▲ U.S. soldiers conduct an exercise using laser attachments that register a hit or miss when they fire at the "enemy" forces opposing them.

▼ The technologically advanced Legged Squad Support System can carry up to 100 pounds/45 kg for 20 miles/32 km before refueling.

systems, an individual can bring down air strikes of enormous power and precision, with just a radio call or trackpad click.

In terms of the future, engineers are experimenting with exoskeletons and even with robots. The future soldier might not even be a human being...

AFTERWORD

In the Introduction to this book, I noted how the art of soldiering is a matter of both continuity and change. Having now journeyed through nearly three centuries of military history, we can give a little precision to these categories.

The greatest revolutions in practical soldiering lie in three main areas: firepower, communications, and transportation. Think back to the soldiers of the Seven Years' War, who traveled around their theaters principally on foot, supported by horse logistics, at best covering distances of about 15 miles/24 km a day. Battlefield communications were conducted verbally, visually, and audibly (and by written message for slower communications), and depended on proximity—soldiers generally had to be physically close to their leaders to take direction. Then, think about firepower. Although the weapons of the 18th century were a pale shadow of what a modern soldier can now deliver, we must still give them respect. We need only to reflect on the huge casualty figures of the major battles of the Seven Years' War and Napoleonic Wars to know that individual weapons might be cumbersome but cumulatively they could do enormous human damage. Nevertheless, this damage was done as much in spite of the technology as because of it.

In the final chapter of this book, we brought the technological picture of soldiering up to date. The transformations noted are huge. Today's soldier can travel hundreds of miles in a day (thanks to vehicular and airborne transportation), can communicate instantly with headquarters on the other side of the globe, and can deliver firepower from an individual's weaponry that would rival that of an entire platoon 200 years ago.

So is soldiering now more about mastering technology than it is about the character and discipline emphasized in the past? It would be lazy simply to say "no." Some fundamental aspects of being a soldier do appear to have changed. For example, many veteran training officers say that soldiers of, say, the 1940s and 50s were generally used to physical hardship in civilian life, so adjusted more easily to a spartan barracks existence than do today's generation, accustomed to more creature comforts. At a more political level, it appears that today's modern armies are no longer willing to accept the dizzying casualty levels of previous centuries. During World War II, for example, a British combat battalion could have lost more men in one month of action than all British forces have lost in over a decade of deployment to Afghanistan.

But we still cannot say that being a modern soldier is a "soft" option compared with the past. The trauma and responsibility of combat is experienced in just the same way by the individual today as it was 70 years ago. Logistics and military administration remain complex businesses, even with the utilization of computer systems. Indeed, some would argue that advanced technology can make managing armed forces more, not less, complicated. Ultimately, soldiering is, and has always been, about individuals and units enduring tough conditions and making judicious decisions, regardless of the tools at their disposal.

CHRIS MCNAB

▶ A British soldier of the Queens Royal Hussars conducts a patrol alongside a soldier from the 51st Brigade, Iraqi Army, Basra, 2009.

INDEX

ACKNOWLEDGEMENTS

With thanks to these picture agencies for permission to publish their images. Front endpaper © Hulton-Deutsch Collection/Corbis; pp1 © Scott Olson/Getty; 2–3 © Fotosearch/Getty; 5 © Heritage Images/Getty; 6 © Hulton Archive/Getty; 8 © Don Troiani/Corbis; 10t © ullstein bild/Getty; 10b © Peter Newark's Military Pictures/Bridgeman; 11t © Mary Evans/Interfoto/Hermann Historica GmbH; 12t © The Stapleton Collection/Bridgeman; 12b © Brown University USA/Bridgeman; 13b © Don Troiani/Corbis; 14t © The Print Collector/Corbis; 14b © Musee Conde/Bridgeman; 15 © Mary Evans/Interfoto; 16 © Look and Learn/Bridgeman; 18b © Mary Evans; 18t © adoc-photos/Corbis; 19 © Print Collector/Getty; 20t © Buyenlarge/Getty; 20b © Universal Images Group/Getty; 21t © Time & Life Pictures/Getty; 21bl © Ed Eckstein/Corbis; 21br © Tim Tadder/Corbis; 22t © Mary Evans Picture Library/Grosvenor Prints; 22b © Mary Evans Picture Library; 25 © Private Collection/Bridgeman; 26t © Mary Evans Picture Library; 24b © Don Troiani/Corbis; 25 © Don Troiani/Corbis; 26 © Don Troiani/Corbis; 28t © US National Archives; 29t © GraphicaArtis/Corbis; 29b © Joseph Sohm/Corbis; 30t © Don Troiani/Corbis; 30b © Don Troiani/Corbis; 31 © Print Collector/Getty; 32 Don Troiani/Corbis; 33 © Mary Evans/Everett Collection; 34 © Louis S Glanzman/Getty; 35 © Don Troiani/Corbis; 36 © Ted Spiegel/Corbis; 37t © DEA Picture Library/Getty; 37b © Baldwin H Ward & Kathryn C Ward/Corbis; 38 © Don Troiani/Corbis; 39t © Corbis; 39b © Bob Krist/Corbis; 40t © Tim Laman/National Geographic Creative/Corbis; 41 © Mary Evans/Library of Congress; 42t © Corbis; 42b © adoc-photos/Corbis; 43b © Stocktrek Images/Corbis; 43t © Lebrecht Music & Arts/Corbis; 44t © Corbis; 44b © Louis S Glanzman/Getty; 45t © National Geographic Creative/Corbis; 45b © Corbis; 46t © Universal Images Group/Getty; 46b © Mary Evans; 46m © Photo Researchers/Mary Evans; 48 © Bogdan Willewalde; 50t © DEA/M Seemuller/Getty; 50b © Stapleton Collection/Corbis; 51t © DEA/A Dagli Orti/Getty; 51b © Don Troiani/Corbis; 53 © Heritage Images/Getty; 54 © Peter John Dickson/Getty; 55 © Michael Nicholson/Corbis; 57t © Dimitry Fomin/Getty; 57b © Don Troiani/Corbis; 58 © Bonhams/Bridgeman; 59 © Mary Evans/Grosvenor Prints; 60t © Wiktor Dabkowski/ZUMA Press/Corbis; 60b © Yuri Kochetkov/epa/Corbis; 61 © Stefano Bianchetti/Corbis; 62t © Photo 12/Getty; 62b © Popperfoto/Getty; 64t © Hulton Archive/Getty; 64b © Mary Evans; 65 © Mary Evans/CAGP/Iberfoto; 66b © DEA/G Dagli Orti/Getty; 67t © Jean Claude Labbe/Getty; 67b © Marco Di Lauro/Getty; 68t © Di Agostini Picture Library/Getty; 68b © Mary Evans; 69 © Roger Viollet Collection/Getty; 70t © Hulton Archive/Getty; 70b © Print Collector/Getty; 71t © Hulton Archive/Getty; 71b © Universal Images Group/Getty; 72 © Mary Evans; 74 © Hulton-Deutsch Collection/Corbis; 76 © US National Archives; 78 © US National Archives; 79t © US National Archives; 80b © US National Archives; 80b © US National Archives; 81 © Buyenlarge/Getty; 82t © JW Petty/Corbis; 82b © US National Archives; 84t © US National Archives; 85t © Medford Historical Society Collection/Corbis; 85b © Corbis; 86 © Buyenlarge/Getty; 87b © Buyenlarge/Getty; 88t © Don Troiani/Corbis; 88b © George Houghton/Vermont Historical Society; 90t © Corbis; 90b © Nigel Partridge; 91t © Hulton-Deutsch/Corbis; 91b © Photo Quest/Getty; 92 © US National Archives; 93t © US National Archives; 93b © Henry P Moore/Corbis; 94b © Corbis; 95 © Corbis; 96 © Mary Evans/David Lewis Hodgson; 97 © Medford Historical Society Collection/Corbis; 88 © Hulton Archive/Getty; 100t © Illustrated London News/Mary Evans; 100b © Print Collector/Getty; 101 © Lebrecht Music & Arts/Corbis; 102 © Universal History Archive/Getty; 103 © Photo 12/Getty; 104t © Hulton-Deutsch Collection/Corbis; 104b © Print Collector/Getty; 105 © Mary Evans/John Maclellan; 106t © Reinhold Thiele/Getty; 106b © Universal Images Group/Getty; 107m © Getty; 107r © Universal Images Group/Getty; 108 © Hulton Archives/Getty; 109 © Hulton Archive/Getty; 110 © Michael Nicholson/Corbis; 111 © Mary Evans/Interfoto; 112t © CS Fly/Corbis; 112b © Culture Club/Getty; 113 © The Print Collector/Corbis; 114t © Hulton-Deutsch Collection/Corbis; 114b © Hulton-Deutsch Collection/Corbis; 115t © Hulton-Deutsch Collection/Corbis; 115b © Africa Media Online/Mary Evans; 116t © Corbis; 116bl © Medford Historical Society Collection/Corbis; 116br © Sovfoto/Getty; 117 © Sovfoto/Getty; 117b © Joe Raedle/Getty; 118t © Mary Evans/Sueddeutsche Zeitung; 118b © Mary Evans/Sueddeutsche Zeitung; 119 © Interfoto/Sammlung Rauch/Mary Evans; 120t © Illustrated London News Ltd/Mary Evans; 120b © Print Collector/Getty; 121 © Print Collector/Getty; 122 © Hulton Archive/Getty; 124b © Photo 12/Getty; 124t © US National Archives; 125t © DEA/Seemuller/Getty; 125b © Underwood & Underwood/Corbis; 126b © Tarker/Corbis; 127 © Leemage/Corbis; 128 © Interfoto/Daniel/Mary Evans; 130 © Lebrecht Music & Arts/Corbis; 131t © Roger Fenton/Getty; 131b © Roger Fenton/Getty; 132 © DEA/G Dagli Orti/Getty; 134b © DEA/G Dagli Orti/Getty; 134t © DEA/G Dagli Orti/Getty; 135 © Frederick Moore/National Geographic Creative/Corbis; 136t © US National Archives; 138t Everett Collection/Mary Evans; 138b © Popperfoto/Getty; 139t © Photo Quest/Getty; 139b © Scott Peterson/Getty; 140t © Hulton Archive/Getty; 140b © Universal Images Group/Getty; 141 © Corbis; 142–3 © LIFE Picture Collection/Getty; 144 © Hulton-Deutsch Collection/Corbis; 146t © Hulton Archive/Getty; 146b © FPG/Getty; 147t © US National Archives; 147b © Popperfoto/Getty; 148b © Hulton Archive/Corbis; 149t © Topical Press Agency/Getty; 150t © Popperfoto/Getty; 150b © IWM/Getty; 151b © Topical Press Agency/

Getty; 152l © US National Archives; 152t © ND/Getty; 152–3 © ND/Getty; 154 © Hulton Archive/Getty; 155t © Mary Evans/Robert Hunt Collection; 155b © Culture Club/Getty; 156b © Corbis; 156t © LIFE Picture Collection/Getty; 157b © Archives/Getty; 158b © Paul Thompson/FPG/Getty; 158t © Branger/Getty; 159 © Hulton Archive/Getty; 160 © Hulton Archive/Corbis; 161t © Hulton Archive/Getty; 161b © Berliner Verlag/Archiv/dpa/Corbis; 162t © Buyenlarge/Getty; 162b © Steven St John/National Geographic/Getty; 163t © Popperfoto/Getty; 163m © Windmill Books/Getty; 163b © Marco di Lauro/Getty; 165t © Bettmann/Corbis; 165b © Bettmann/Corbis; 167 © Hulton Archive/Getty; 168 © Everett Collection/Getty; 170 © Hulton Archive/Getty; 170 © Corbis; 171 © Joseph Schwartz/Corbis; 173 © Bettmann/Corbis; 174t © Hulton Archive/Getty; 174b © Bettmann/Corbis; 174–5 © Berliner Verlag/Archiv/dpa/Corbis; 176 © Sovfoto/Getty; 177t © Berliner Verlag/Archiv; 177b © Berliner Verlag/Archiv; 178t © FPG/Getty; 178b © Roger Viollet/Getty; 179 © Nigel Dobinson/Getty; 181t © Bettmann/Corbis; 181m © Keystone/Getty; 181b © Berliner Verlag/Archiv/dpa/Corbis; 182 © Mary Evans/SZ Photo/Scherl; 183 © Hulton Archive/Getty; 184t © Underwood Archives/Getty; 184b © Fox Photos/Getty; 187t © Asahi Shimbun/Getty; 187b © Corbis; 188bl © Mary Evans/Alexander Meledin; 188br © Sovfoto/Getty; 189t © Mary Evans/Alexander Meledin; 189b © Marco di Lauro/Getty; 190 © Hulton Archive/Getty; 190b © Popperfoto/Getty; 191 © LIFE Picture Collection/Getty; 192t © Pictorial Parade/Getty; 192b © John Florea/LIFE Picture Collection/Getty; 193 © Keystone/Getty; 194t © Corbis; 194b © W Eugene Smith/LIFE Picture Collection/Getty; 196 © US Army/Getty; 198 © Keystone-France Pictures/Getty; 199t © Rolls Press/Popperfoto/Getty; 199b © David Furst/AFP/Getty; 200t Picture Post/Getty; 200b © Keystone/Getty; 201b © Keystone-France/Getty; 202 © Bettmann/Corbis; 203 © AFP/Getty; 205 © Terry Fincher/Getty; 206t © Getty; 206b © Vittoriano Rastelli/Corbis; 207 © Mondadori Portfolio/Getty; 208t © Jose Nicolas/Corbis; 208b © Antoine Gyori/Sygma/Corbis; 210t © Chris Hondros/Getty; 210b © John D McHugh/Getty; 211 © ullstein bild Pictures/Getty; 212b © Mary Evans/Alexander Meledin; 212t © Mary Evans; 213t © Pacific Press/Getty; 213b © Robert Nickelsberg/Getty; 215t © Filippo Monteforte/Getty; 215tr © Ahmad Al-Rubaye/Getty; 215b © Nicolas Asfouri/Getty; 216 © Mike Nelson/Getty; 217t © MCT/Getty; 217b © Boston Globe/Getty; 219 © Matt Cardy/Getty; back endpaper © David H Wells/Corbis.

This edition published by Parragon Books Ltd in 2016

Parragon Books Ltd
Chartist House
15–17 Trim Street
Bath BA1 1HA, UK
www.parragon.com

Copyright © Parragon Books Ltd 2016

Produced by Joanne Rippin
Illustrated by Simon Smith and Matthew Vince
Stylings and design by Nigel Partridge

All rights reserved. No part of this publication may be reproduced, stored in a retrieval system or transmitted, in any form or by any means, electronic, mechanical, photocopying, recording or otherwise, without the prior permission of the copyright holder.

ISBN 978-1-4748-0417-2

. Printed in China